...UCK'S

Wild Tracks

More **Wild Tracks**

Trevor Fishlock

seren

seren is the book imprint of
Poetry Wales Press Ltd
Nolton Street, Bridgend, CF31 3BN, Wales
www.seren-books.com

Book based on the HTV Wales series 'Fishlock's Wild Tracks'
produced by Ffilmiau'r Nant

Published with the kind permission of HTV Wales Ltd

© Trevor Fishlock, 2000. Reprinted 2001

ISBN 1-85411-292-9

A CIP record for this title is available from
the British Library

*The publisher works with the financial assistance of the
Arts Council of Wales*

Maps by Lorraine Bewsey

Printed in Plantin by Gomer Press, Llandysul

Contents

Introduction

For the past six years I have spent the month of May walking the hills and valleys of Wales. It is a wonderful time. The light has a quality that makes artists reach for their brushes. The bluebells carpet the woods, the leaves are young and the whole landscape looks freshly-painted. In other words, it is the perfect time for the *Fishlock's Wild Tracks* team to shoulder the tripod and take to the mountain paths, the cliffs, beaches, moors, zigzag lanes and village streets.

By now this annual expedition has for us taken on the character of an enjoyable pilgrimage. Each walk, each programme, leads us into a new stretch of countryside with magnificent views and a store of surprises.

It gives us great pleasure to read and research the background of the districts we visit and to listen to the stories told by local people, all part of the *Wild Tracks* mixture of history, humour, local voices and beautiful landscapes.

We are always struck by the richness of each district and the pride that its people have in it. And we love to unearth the stories that leave even the most knowledgeable locals saying: 'Well, I've lived here all these years and I never knew that.'

One thing is clear: Wales is not at all monolithic. Each valley, village, neighbourhood and bro has its own distinctive quality and voice. Every May, when we apply our boots to the track, we are astonished and delighted by the sheer variety of the country.

Many people have remarked to me that we always seem to have sunny weather when we are walking. Certainly I have to take care not to get a sunburnt nose. The fact that I do not wear a coat when the camera is turning adds to the illusion that Wales is as blessed with abundant sunshine as a Mediterranean island.

Well, there are six half-hour programmes in each series and each takes four days to film; and we would be very lucky indeed to get 24 sunny days in the month. The truth is, of course, that we have to chase the sunshine and are devoted and anxious listeners to the weather forecasts. Wil Aaron, the programme's director, has added meteorology to his many skills and is an uncanny predictor of sunny spells.

In every part of Wales people say – or boast – that their particular district has its own private climate; and it is true that on days when much of the country is grey and rainy we are often lucky to find ourselves basking in our own spotlight of sunshine.

Nevertheless, it can be very cold in May on Welsh hills and my outward show of shirtsleeve courage often conceals a vital shield of thin but thermal underwear.

We have established a pattern in each *Wild Tracks* series of making two programmes in the north, two in the middle and two in the south. This, the second *Wild Tracks* book, reflects that pattern and its twelve chapters take in Pembrokeshire, the Garw Valley, Caernarfonshire, Gwent, Radnorshire, Flintshire, the Sirhowy Valley, the Vale of Glamorgan, Lleyn, the Vyrnwy Valley and the Vale of Clwyd.

I am sure that all the people who watch the programmes can tell how much Wil Aaron and the production team and I enjoy making them. That enjoyment is reflected in this book. Here, once again, land and people, is Wales speaking entertainingly for itself.

Trevor Fishlock

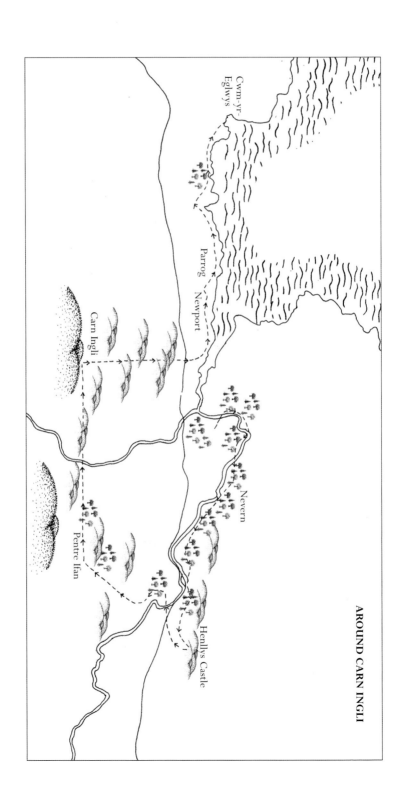

AROUND CARN INGLI

Cwm-yr-Eglwys

Parrog
Newport

Carn Ingli

Neven

Pentre Ifan

Henllys Castle

1. AROUND CARN INGLI

The enchanted mountain and the Japanese garden

For a dozen years or so, I have spent a few days in winter with friends in the little Pembrokeshire town of Newport, on a bay along the coast between Fishguard and Cardigan. Trefdraeth is its Welsh name, the town on the sands.

On the first day of every year, snow or sunshine, I have made a point, a personal pilgrimage, of climbing out of town, past the church and the castle, to the top of Carn Ingli mountain. More often than not a blustery wind hisses through the gorse. It slaps at my face as I make the exciting scramble up the grey rocky outcrop of the summit. It is as if I am being made to pay a price for my intrusion. Sometimes rain and dark clouds have bullied me off the top; but I have also experienced many wonderful sharp sunny days, a midwinter preview of spring.

For a *Wild Tracks* walk around Carn Ingli, however, I chose May and started on the main road at Llwyngwair Lodge. It is an irresistible curiosity, a charming teapot of a house, with its rooms

Theatre in the round: Mrs Davies's famous circular tours

built around its central chimney. I was invited in by Doris Davies, the owner, who, on certain days, shows people around to raise money for a cancer charity. For the fun of it, she dresses the part in a nineteenth-century costume of shawl and a black bonnet.

As she took me up the corkscrew stairs I asked her if she ever felt dizzy; and she said no, although her nephew refers to her as 'My giddy aunt.'

Fortified by her tea and fruit cake, I walked the footpath through tranquil wooded countryside, following the River Nevern along part of its course from the Preseli Hills to Newport Bay.

The track into the village of Nevern has been a pilgrims' way

for centuries, trodden by people marching to St David's to worship at the saint's bones. Beside the path I found a cross, scratched into a rock, where pilgrims paused to pray, topping up their tanks of faith. More than a thousand years ago the coast of Pembrokeshire was the heart of a busy pioneer Christian community and many chapels were built where Celtic saints and missionaries landed.

Pray stop: the pilgrims' cross on the path to Nevern

The church at Nevern is one of nine in south-western Wales dedicated to St Brynach. He was a cult figure in his day. He narrowly avoided seduction by a princess and escaped being driven mad by demons before settling quietly at Nevern. The church tower dates from the twelfth century and in the churchyard is a famous Celtic cross, 13 feet high, ornately-carved and about ten centuries old. A legend says that on the first day of spring a cuckoo perched upon it to call people to prayer. However, I found someone much more reliable than the flighty cuckoo: Megan James, the cheerful bellringer. She gave me a demonstration, tugging the bell strings in the manner of a milk-maid pulling at the udders of a cow.

The parish records show that in 1667 the local people

Cuckoo's rest: Nevern's Celtic stone

contributed nearly two pounds for the relief of the poor after the Great Fire of London and more than 30 shillings to help Christian slaves in Turkey. I wonder how the money got there.

A similar spirit of generosity inspired a Nevern man who prospered as a draper in London. In his will, in 1806, he left a sum of money to pay for an annual dinner of beef and barley for some of the villagers. The trustees of the legacy supervise the division of the joint into about ten pieces, and they themselves eat the rest at a jolly lunch. The meat was never intended to feed the poor, which is just as well, for Nevern folk are peckish rather than hungry. Of late, Megan James the bellringer has cooked the beef, playing her part in fulfilling the generous draper's legacy of fellowship, simple pleasure and laughter.

I rejoined the path beside the meandering river and strode into Felindre Farchog. The foursquare Welsh chapel, staunch, honest and devoid of vanity, sets an example to its congregation.

Climbing the track towards Henllys Castle I found strips of cloth tied to the branches above my head. They reminded me of the prayer papers I have seen fluttering in Japanese temples. Such pieces of cloth were the traditional symbols of prayers offered to the Celtic gods believed to inhabit ancient wells.

Guardian of the spring

Beside the spring at the top of the path I found crudely-carved little statues, standing like sentries. These and the strips of cotton and wool have been put here recently to help the 8,000 children who visit Henllys every year to imagine the lives of their ancestors who lived in the Iron Age, more than two thousand years ago. The giant thatched wigwams I saw faithfully replicate those built on this very site by Iron Age settlers. I watched as the faces of dozens of children were daubed with blue woad. It all helped to bring the past vividly alive.

Heading south-west, I crossed the A487 and made my way to even more remote times, following the finger-post pointing to Pentre Ifan. This cromlech, with its 17-foot capstone, is one of the dramatic sights of Britain. It was the gateway to a great tomb erected by people who arrived in Pembrokeshire five thousand

Great gaunt stones summon up our distant past

years ago, probably by sea. Standing beside this enigmatic remnant I found it easy to imagine the great chieftains who roamed and ruled the region and were laid to rest on this windswept hill.

Yet all of the landscape of Pembrokeshire has a rich residue of legends. I walked for a while with Brian John, the historian and storyteller, who was long ago bewitched by Pembrokeshire and has written many books about it. 'There used to be a tradition of hauling corpses up the chimney,' he said. 'The body was wrapped in a sheet and a rope was fed down the chimney and attached to it. The corpse was pulled up the chimney to allow the spirit to escape and was then lowered to be placed in a coffin.'

The charm of Pembrokeshire, its distance and beauty, small meadows and farms, has always drawn people who dream of fulfilment, working the land, seeking a simpler life, and a living, in the hills. Julian Orbach is one of them. He believes you can combine flowers in the meadows and efficiency; that he and his family can live well on a small hill farm without ploughing big money into machinery. He was using a horse to work the land. He showed me the animal house he built, a circular building with a turf roof. When the grass grows long his goats jump onto the roof and nibble it down to tidiness. Julian was gradually dispensing with mains electricity and used a windmill to capture the breeze and transform it into electric light.

Rooftop restaurant   Gateway to a simpler life

I walked up the narrow road to the farm, high on Carn Ingli, which has been run for more than half a century by bachelor brothers William John and Dewi Jenkins. They sat me down in their kitchen and poured tea. As they talked I felt I had not often met men so in tune with their landscape. Independent, good-humoured and with ready laughter, they've been here all their lives, making a living in the old-fashioned way on their few rugged acres. They've never had a holiday, never ventured far from this hillside, never been to London.

'Why should we?' asked William John with a smile. 'Everything we want is here.'

For more than fifty years they have compiled a diary, sitting every evening to record in Welsh the storms and droughts, the fortunes of their farm, the lost sheep, the deaths of friends and neighbours, and the celebrations of marriages and births: M for marwolaeth, death; P for priodas, wedding; A for angladd, funeral; and G for genedigaeth, birth.

Their diary chronicles lives of hard work and celebrates a way of life on the windbitten slopes. The mountain is also their inspiration, for in this district the brothers are famous for the songs they write; and they sang one for me ... 'Carn Ingli, I love you' ... to send me on my way.

The volcanic ramparts of the mountain command the land. To some these heights are haunted and magical, an abode of gods.

St Brynach's domain: from the top of Carn Ingli

Tradition relates that St Brynach, the patron saint of this district, would climb up here to be closer to heaven. The top is a natural fortress and from the battlements I had a magnificent view over the Preseli Hills and down to Dinas Head.

Newport Castle: walls have years

At my feet nestled Newport. Amiable and steeped in antiquity, it has had a charter and a mayor for almost eight hundred years. The people are proud of their links to medieval times. Twice every year, in keeping with tradition, the Lord of Cemais, the major landowner in the district, presides over a court where the mayor and burgesses discuss town business. The title of Lord of Cemais originated in the struggles of the Norman Conquest and the present holder, Hyacinthe Hawkesworth, still has certain feudal powers.

In the Baptist chapel I paused to listen to the unforgettable sound of another tradition: the Pwnc. Men, women and children gather to chant New Testament verses to an extraordinary rhythm. It began as a way of teaching people to memorise the scriptures. 'Pwnc is about 150 years old,' said the Reverend Alwyn Daniels. 'The chapels compete in a Pwnc festival and each has a different and distinctive sound. It is a special part of this district's Christian heritage.'

Walking out of town, by way of the Parrog, I passed the pink cottage where once the limekiln keeper used to live, and followed the twisting thread of the Pembrokeshire coastal path. Below me stretched the bay, once busy with schooners. There used to be horse racing on the great flat pan of Newport sands. In August of 1862 the Reverend Evan Lewis prayed in chapel that God should show displeasure at such sin. At that moment, so they say, horses fell at one of the hurdles and jockeys were injured.

I walked the embroidered petticoats of Wales, the clifftops brilliant with the pink of squill and thrift, ruffled by the wind. Far below, the green sea exploded into dazzling surf on the rocks and promontories.

I made my way into Cwm-yr-Eglwys. The wall standing close to the shore is all that survives of the twelfth-century church. It was smashed during the terrible storm of 1859 when more than a hundred ships were wrecked along the western coast of Wales.

Defiant stones: Cwm-yr-Eglwys church

You might think the hamlet a perfect hideaway. Certainly a woman called Edith May Hallowell Carew thought so. She moved into a cottage in the 1930s. Over the years she planted a Japanese garden, the remains of which I was shown. It was the only clue to a terrible chapter in her life. I heard the story from Vernon Jones.

'She was convicted of murdering her husband in Yokohama in 1897 and sentenced to death. But the Emperor of Japan commuted the sentence to life imprisonment. She served part of it in Hong Kong and the rest in England.'

Her husband, an Englishman, died of arsenic poisoning. There was a suggestion that he may have used arsenic himself to treat his venereal disease. Whatever the truth, Edith May herself never spoke of the matter. After her release from prison she journeyed to remote Cwm-yr-Eglwys to escape her past and find peace. She died there in 1958.

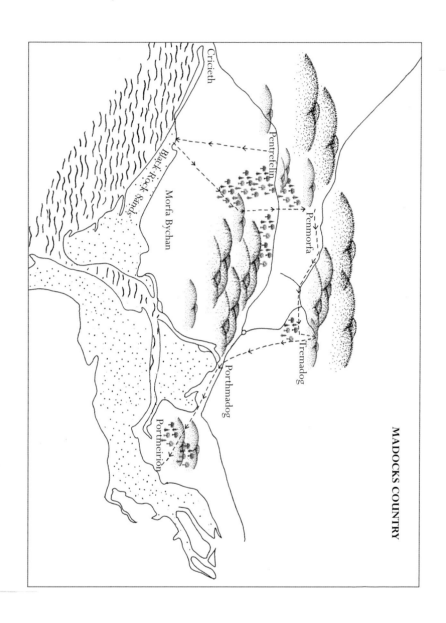

MADOCKS COUNTRY

Cricieth

Black Rock Sands

Morfa Bychan

Pentrefelin

Penmorfa

Tremadog

Porthmadog

Portmeirion

2. MADOCKS COUNTRY

The land of dreams

The heart of this walk, from Pentrefelin to Portmeirion, was Madocks country, the landscape and places associated with William Alexander Madocks, man of vision, action and business; and one of the most remarkable figures of nineteenth-century Wales. He was a heroic romantic. He gave up his career as a Member of Parliament and devoted his life to a glorious but unsuccessful attempt to fulfil his dream of opening a road from London to north Wales. To this end he built the handsome little town of Tremadog and much of its larger sibling, Porthmadog.

But I am getting ahead of myself. I started walking at Pentrefelin, a village on the road from Cricieth to Porthmadog, and soon came to a tall stone by the roadside which, like a policeman's admonishing finger, seemed to command me to stop. It had a date carved on it, 1721, but that was all. Something happened in 1721 but no-one remembers what.

Search the history books and you will see that 1721 was a dull year for events. But 1752 was full of excitement. That was the year

The stone with no name

the government reformed the calendar in Britain, simply doing away with eleven days. Wednesday September 2 that year was followed by Thursday September 14. The people of Pentrefelin were mightily confused – they were not the only ones – and they could not work out when it was Christmas Day. Being properly sceptical, they would not take the government's word for it. They sent Shon Evan Griffith, the village miller's brother, on a mission to Glastonbury in Somerset. There, it was believed, the thorn planted by Joseph of Arimathea flowered on Christmas morning. Shon walked to Glastonbury and returned months later. Well? said the villagers, all agog. Oh yes, said Shon, the thorn flowered on December 25 and the new calendar was all right. Shon was a local hero, the man who found Christmas.

I passed by Hendregadredd, the house which gives its name to a great collection of medieval poetry. The Hendregadredd Manuscript is a parchment volume of verses written mostly in the fourteenth century and includes a poem by the great Dafydd ap Gwilym. Many scholars believe that part of it is in his own hand. The manuscript was lost around the beginning of the nineteenth century and rediscovered in 1910 in a wardrobe at Hendregadredd. In 1923, the wealthy Davies sisters of Gregynog used some of their

Flanker: Moel-y-Gest

family's coal fortune and bought it for the National Library of Wales. It is the sort of story that makes people go upstairs to check the wardrobe.

With the bulk of Moel Hebog guarding my back, Tremadog rocks and Moel-y-Gest on my flank, I headed for the little church at Ynyscynhaiarn. This was once an island in a lagoon, but the water has long since receded, leaving the church a castaway in a sea of green meadows.

Ynyscynhaiarn: White Rock, Jack Black

In the churchyard, as always, the stones tell their stories. On the right, as I walked up the path, was the grave of the harpist David Owen, better known as Dafydd y Garreg Wen, David of the White Rock, the name of the haunting Welsh air. It is said that Dafydd composed it as he lay dying and it was first played at his funeral. I noticed that, 250 years on, admirers still leave tributes of wild flowers on his grave.

On the left of the churchyard, I pushed aside the ferns concealing the stone over the grave of the remarkable Jack Black, who died in 1791. The Welsh verse

> Yn India gynna'm ganwyd,– a nghamrau
> Ynghymru'm bedyddiwyd ...

says he came from India and was baptised in Wales; but the first line is poetic licence. Eryl Rothwell Hughes, who told me the story, said that Jack Black, also called John Ystumllyn, was about eight years old when one of the Wynne family brought him from Africa to Ystumllyn, near Cricieth. That was around 1746. We can only imagine how frightened he must have been at first. He was brought up in the Wynne household, learnt Welsh and English and became an excellent gardener.

He was very attractive to young women in the neighbourhood and he eventually courted Margaret Gruffydd, a maidservant. They married in Dolgellau and Jack's best man was the son of the vicar of Cricieth. The couple had seven children and the family used to worship at Ynyscynhaiarn church. Jack Black's son lived at Llandwrog, became Lord Newborough's huntsman, and worked for him for fifty-six years.

The church boasts a rare three-decker pulpit. Bishops, being closer to heaven, spoke from the top, while vicars and curates preached below. The congregation, meanwhile, was carefully boxed in pews painted, as can still be seen, with the names of the local farms. Masters and servants knew their place in church and society.

The smell of meadows mingled with the scent of the sea as I walked down the path, crossed the railway line and made for Black

Black Rock: 'utterly peculiar...'

Rock Sands. The stone fist of Cricieth Castle, the unmistakable landmark hereabouts, was on my right.

Robert Graves, the poet, spent his childhood holidays across the Glaslyn estuary at Harlech. The beaches and mysterious sea caves of Black Rock excited his imagination and inspired the delightful poem he called *Welsh Incident* which tells of 'Very strange, un-Welsh, utterly peculiar Things'.

I took off my boots and rolled up my trousers and wandered into one of the caves, a narrow labyrinth twisting far into the mountain. Were I a child or a poet I should certainly imagine a monster lurking deep in the heart of it.

Turning inland to the slopes of Moel-y-Gest, I climbed a path that gave me a good view over the sands of Morfa Bychan. The old books tell that what happened down there in 1694 was like the creepier sort of horror film. A strange burning mist with a blue flame in the middle of it rose out of the marshland and floated over the sands as far as Harlech. As it drifted it killed cattle and birds and set fire to hayricks and barns. It was very eerie, a luminous blue cloud that reappeared many times over several months. People started banging drums and blowing horns and firing their guns, as if it were a strange presence that could be frightened away. And in the end it vanished.

Position of strength: Cricieth's knuckles

25

Towards the top of the slope I came to Bron-y-Foel, a house that in medieval times was at the heart of a savage feud. It came to a head when Gruffydd ap John, leading a private army, attacked the house which was defended by his neighbour Hywel ap Rhys. Hywel killed his attacker with a well-aimed arrow fired from a window: it went through the thin gap in his helmet visor. Another owner of this house was Sir Hywel of the Axe who fought with the Black Prince in France in the fourteenth century. He was a useful man to have on your side: with one swipe of his axe he beheaded the horse ridden by the French king. His reward was a plum job, Constable of Cricieth Castle.

On the road to Tremadog I stopped in the churchyard of Penmorfa to look at the grave of Sir John Owen. He fought for the king in the Civil War and to this day is honoured for his courage. I found a group of Sir John's admirers gathered around the tomb, members of The Sealed Knot, the society which re-enacts battles of the Civil War. They were all dressed in costumes of the period and take pride in getting the details right, the uniforms, the weapons, even the food, seeking a better understanding of history by imagining themselves to be soldiers of the mid-seventeenth century.

I listened as one of them, Paul Le Pinnet, playing the part of an officer, told the group of Sir John's virtues. Sir John saw much fighting and was captured near Llandygai. Put on trial with four Cavalier lords, he was condemned to death and told the court that 'it is an honour for a poor Welsh gentleman to have his head cut off in such noble company'. Later, in the House of Commons, Oliver Cromwell's son-in-law noted the efforts made to get reprieves for the four lords, while no-one had spoken up for humble Sir John, who had not even tried to have himself spared. The House agreed that Sir John should live and eventually he returned to Penmorfa, full of honour, and lived to see the monarchy restored.

In the early nineteenth century, William Madocks built his handsome town of Tremadog beneath a great crag on land reclaimed from the sea. It was intended to be an important staging post on the London to Dublin coach road with a hotel to accommodate coach passengers. The Union Inn marked the Act of Union with Ireland in 1800. The Golden Fleece saluted the local wool trade. Madocks built a wool factory with water-powered looms. Unfortunately his dream was never realized. The coach route was built farther north and no stage coaches clattered to Madocks's fine hotel.

Frances Voelcker, who has studied Tremadog's history, described the ingenious design of the town hall. 'It was a market on the ground floor, doubling up as a theatre, and upstairs was the meeting room with a dance floor suspended on chains and where they also held the first school. The houses in the market square were originally shops, an innovation because in those days there was not really such a thing as a shop in north Wales.'

One of the shops in Tremadog was the Cambrian Pill Depot owned by Robert Isaac Jones whose pills were famous in Victorian times and were swallowed for rheumatism and upset stomachs. His Worm Lozenges were popular, too. Kill or cure, I suppose.

Madocks built the splendidly theatrical Methodist chapel in Tremadog and, across the road, a rather plain church. The Bishop of Bangor was displeased that Madocks erected a chapel as well as a church. Madocks sought to calm him down. 'Your Grace, the church is built upon rock, while the chapel rests upon sand.'

Cheerful chapel, Tremadog

One of Madocks's enthusiastic supporters was the poet Percy Bysshe Shelley who stayed with him at his home, Tan-yr-Allt. Perhaps Madocks was delighted to have the company of such a celebrity. Shelley, however, was not popular in the neighbourhood.

Tan-yr-Allt: the poet and the potshot

He was a shocking and scandalous figure; and once came down to dinner stark naked. If, when he was out walking in the hills, he encountered a sheep he thought was unwell he shot it. He stirred up the local workers and failed to pay the butcher and the baker. One night someone took a shot at him, slightly wounding him and making a hole in his nightshirt. That was his story, anyway. Local people thought he made it all up as an excuse to flee without paying his bills.

Henry Archer put his stamp on history while staying in Tremadog. He invented a machine for perforating paper. The Post Office saw at once that this would put an end to the dreary labour of cutting postage stamps with scissors. Archer was paid £4,000 for his invention, which in 1846 was a fortune.

On my way out of the town, I passed Woodlands, the birthplace of Thomas Edward Lawrence, who was to make his name as a remarkable soldier, author and man of mystery. Lawrence of Arabia, as he became, was born in 1888, the illegitimate child of a governess and an Anglo-Irish landowner. The journalist Ivor Wynne Jones told me that through his grandparents Lawrence had a stronger Welsh pedigree than he ever knew.

As part of his master plan Madocks cut a canal, which can still be seen, connecting Tremadog to a new embankment across the River Glaslyn. He used to float down it in a gaily-painted boat. The embankment, known as the Cob, was built between 1808 and

1812 and almost 3,000 acres of land were reclaimed behind it. Gradually, the river scoured out a new harbour at Porthmadog and from the 1860s to the 1880s the town boomed and grew. Its ships carried slates to roof the world. I spent an absorbing hour in the museum which tells the story of the shipping heyday and of the schooners, built by David Jones and David Williams, famous for their turn of speed.

On the edge of the town a path leads up to the Ynys Towyn rocks which afford a magnificent grandstand view of the Cob, the harbour and the distant mountains. Part of the rock is riddled with holes and I learnt that these were the 'rock cannons' that fired salutes on special occasions. Gunpowder was poured into the holes and ignited at intervals to give a dramatic bang-bang-bang effect. They were developed by the quarrymen, who had experience of explosives, as a novel way of celebrating weddings and of welcoming VIPs. Rock cannons were fired to celebrate the completion of the Cob and to welcome Queen Victoria when she travelled up the Ogwen Valley to Bethesda. In 1894 one of the cannon men blew himself up when he absent-mindedly put his pipe in a pocketful of gunpowder.

Cannonade: the rock salute

The northern express

The Cob and the Ffestiniog railway go together. The trains have been running here since 1836. Originally the slate-filled wagons rattled down the line from the quarries, drawn by the force of gravity. Teams of horses, carried in a wagon at the rear, dragged the empty trucks back to the quarries. From 1863 steam locomotives did the job. Years ago a very nervous woman bought a ticket for the train and questioned the guard about what would happen if the carriage couplings snapped. Not to worry, he replied, if that should happen we have the finest brakes. But, she said, not at all reassured, what if the brakes fail? Then, madam, said the guard, it all depends on whether you have lived a good life or a wicked one.

I crossed the Cob, climbed the hill to Penrhyn Isaf Farm, scene of a murder which has stayed in the memory. Nel Thomas sat me down and over tea related the tale. It concerned Thomas Edwards, a labourer who worked on the Cob. He was known as the Hwntw Mawr, the Big Southerner, hwntw being a north Wales term for someone from the south. In September 1812 he entered the farmhouse at Penrhyn Isaf, believing that gold was hidden there. To his surprise he found Mary Jones, the eighteen-year-old farm servant, making cakes. He stabbed her to death. A local posse captured him a few days later. He escaped but was caught again and in 1813, aged sixty-nine, was hanged at Dolgellau jail.

I walked to the highest point of the peninsula to see the standing stone, thin as a needle, which once may have supported a beacon. Up here there is one of the best views in Wales. To the north rises Snowdon; to the east the Moelwyn Range; and, to the south, the rough old Rhinog mountains.

The hamlet down the road used to be called Aber-Iâ. But to Clough Williams-Ellis the name did not have the right ring to it and when he started to build his exotic dream town he gave it a new name: Portmeirion. It was his special genius, his feeling for landscape and buildings, that made Portmeirion so enchanting. He created a theatre; and when you enter you are yourself on stage, a strolling player.

If Clough was an eccentric, he wasn't the first to make his mark on this magical corner, as I heard from Trefor Davies. A botanist who lived here spent a fortune on landscaping. When he went bankrupt he hid from his creditors, staying in his cellar and being fed through a trap door by his loyal butler. We still enjoy his palm trees that flourish in the woods.

In Clough's seaside palace of fun

The last owner of Aber-Iâ, Mrs Adelaide Haigh, disliked people and loved dogs. She had about 40 of them. She erected high screens so that she would not have to see her servants. When her pets died she buried them in a little canine cemetery in the Gwyllt, still in use today. She always refused to cut or trim trees so that when she died the undertaker had to hack his way through the jungle that had grown thickly around the house.

Walking through Portmeirion, I saw that, typically, Sir Clough had his own face carved as a gargoyle, as if he were forever keeping a fond eye upon his entertaining kingdom.

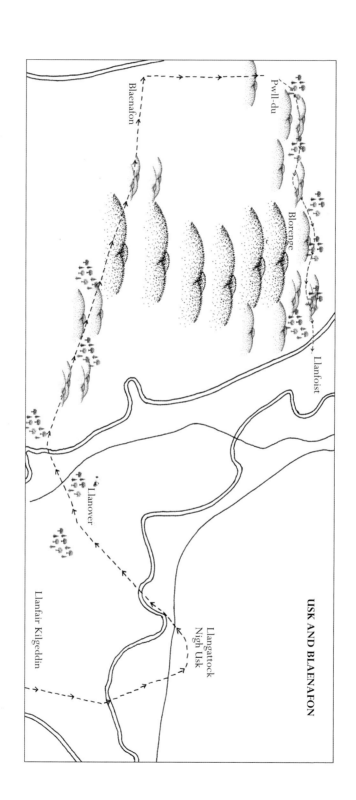

USK AND BLAENAFON

Pwll-du

Blaenafon

Blorenge

Llanfoist

Llanover

Llanfair Kilgeddin

Llangattock
Nigh Usk

3. USK AND BLAENAFON

By way of the golden horse

From the meadowlands of the Usk on a summer's morning I headed west across the wind-whipped moor to see the dramatic remnants of Blaenafon's industrial history. A good forecast and brilliant light promised a day of clear and spectacular views.

Llanfair Kilgeddin: a husband's tribute

Art and love

The church near the Usk at Llanfair Kilgeddin was a beautiful starting point. The interior walls are decorated with remarkable *sgraffito* murals. The artist worked with damp layers of white and coloured plaster, cutting his images deeply to glorious effect.

The Reverend William Lindsay, the vicar, commissioned the murals as a memorial to his wife Rosamond who died in 1885.

Similarly, nearby Clytha Castle is a monument raised by a widower and for that reason is fancifully called a Taj Mahal. William Jones built it in 1790 'for the purpose of relieving a mind sincerely afflicted by grief'.

Clytha Castle: out of sorrow

I walked over one of the handsome stone bridges that are the ornaments of the river to reach St Cadoc's church at Llangattock Nigh Usk. Hywel Griffiths told me the story of a local builder, John Upton, who made some repairs to the church in the 1820s. He ran out of money and fled the country to escape his creditors. He was next heard of in Russia where he worked for the Russian government building the defences at Sebastopol.

'He did a good job,' said Hywel. 'During the Crimean War the fortress at Sebastopol held up the British advance for six months.'

The old rectory, Penpergwm House, is now a home for the elderly. In the 1930s the pianist Dame Myra Hess used to stay here with her friend the rector's wife, and naturally she played the piano, her music drifting on the summer air.

It is not surprising that in Llanover there's still a sense of the dominating presence of Augusta Waddington Hall, better known as Lady Llanover. In every way this remarkable nineteenth-century enthusiast for Welsh culture lived up to her grand and imperious

Christian name. Ever busy, she also lived up to the bardic name she gave herself: Gwenynen Gwent, the Bee of Gwent.

'In many ways she was ahead of her time,' said Sian Rhiannon Williams, who has studied her life. 'She was passionate about Wales and the Welsh language and made the Abergavenny district a thriving Welsh cultural centre.'

Lady Llanover amassed an important collection of Welsh manuscripts, now in the National Library in Aberystwyth. She built a woollen mill to make cloth for the 'traditional' costumes she designed, and a workshop to make harps. She did not know much Welsh herself, but she ran a thoroughly Welsh household, employed only Welsh-speakers and always had a harpist on her staff.

Dry days in Llanover

She was an indefatigable campaigner against alcohol and turned the pubs on her estate into tea shops or private houses. The Nag's Head became the post office, but the original inn sign hangs there to this day. Someone composed the cheeky doggerel:

> Grand house, but small cheer,
> Large cellar but no beer,
> Lord Llanover lives here.

Lord Llanover, formerly Benjamin Hall MP, was Commissioner

of Works in London and his nickname was given to the most famous clock in the world: Big Ben. In Wales he is also remembered as a reformer. He dissociated himself from the Established Church and supported the right of people to have services in Welsh. He also campaigned against the truck shops, the notorious company stores which many employers insisted their workers should use.

Lady Llanover died in 1896 at the age of ninety-four and was escorted to her grave by 20 young women dressed in the costumes she had invented for Wales. She was laid to rest beside her husband, and the grand tomb is one of the sights of Llanover churchyard.

'She was both loved and hated,' Sian Rhiannon Williams told me. 'In Llanover she was sometimes called "the mother of us all". But there was no doubt she was authoritarian and imposed her will.'

I called at the small chapel in the village which is called Hanover in gratitude to the Hanoverian kings of England who gave nonconformists greater freedom of worship. On the wall at the far end is a memorial to an intrepid young local man, Robert Thomas. He was the first Protestant missionary to the then little-known country of Korea. He was killed there in 1866 while distributing bibles. Modern Korean Christians salute him as a martyr; and hundreds of them make a pilgrimage here every year. 'Bless Wales,' they write in the visitors' book. 'Bless Wales for blessing Korea.'

A short walk brought me to the memorial to the 21 young men of Llanover killed in the First World War. One was Lady Llanover's grandson, Elidyr. The estate planted a grove of trees, one for each dead soldier, and around a green built a house for each life lost.

The path took me over the Monmouthshire and Brecon Canal, one of the transport arteries of the nineteenth century, and past the Goose and Cuckoo pub. It was just outside Lady Llanover's estate, so she didn't get her teetotal hands on it.

On the way up to the moors I came across an odd-looking conical construction, a sort of stone igloo. I didn't know what it was, so I consulted the Reverend Anthony Parkinson, who has expert knowledge of such buildings.

'It's a pig sty,' he told me, 'of a kind you only see in south Wales. There's a tradition of drystone building in this part of the world, and it is easier to build a drystone wall that does not have

Porkers' palace

corners. It is a very old technique ... such circular buildings were constructed in Wales in pre-Roman times.'

I crawled in through the small entrance. Inside it was dry and cosy. Centuries ago the pigs of Wales lived in some comfort.

High up on the moor I reached the halfway point of my walk, a clear boundary, the Usk on one side and the Lwyd on the other. I looked behind me at the soft green eiderdown of the Usk Valley and headed over the bleak and shelterless land towards the industrial valley. I stopped at the isolated place where the noble horse Foxhunter lies buried. In the 1952 Olympic Games he did what no mere man could do: he brought home Britain's only gold medal. In 1999 the ashes of Sir Harry Llewellyn, who rode Foxhunter to victory, were scattered over the grave.

Blaenafon is one of the starting places of modern industrial history. Indeed, archaeologists and historians believe that the story of the industrial revolution is told more completely around here than anywhere in the world. Blaenafon set the pace. The heart of it all is the massive ironworks, the place of roaring fire, where men, women and children laboured in brutal conditions. Blast furnaces, with air blown into them by steam engines, the very latest technology, started working in 1789. Within seven years Blaenafon was the second largest ironworks in Wales, after Merthyr.

I wandered the awesome remnants of the furnaces and kilns and

Land of fire: furnace at Blaenafon

Iron rule: even the tombs have iron lids

gazed up at the great water balance tower, an hydraulic lift, built in 1839. Though silent now, the ruins speak eloquently of the years of fire, thunderous noise, power and human suffering. We know something of the people who worked here from the report of a commission on child labour in the 1840s. The father of Timothy and Thomas Macarthy, aged nine and seven, told the inspectors his boys were fourteen and ten. He was afraid that if the truth got out they would lose their jobs. As it was, he said, they worked 12-hour night shifts and enjoyed them.

In the iron age of Blaenafon babies were baptised in an iron font in St Peter's church and many graves were marked not by stone but by iron. Ashes to ashes, rust to rust. Among the iron tombs I found that of Thomas Deakin who ran the iron ore mines for many years. He had started working at the age of nine, hauling coal trucks in Shropshire with a chain around his waist, a pony in human form.

The experience haunted him all his days. 'I would not allow my children to work as I did,' he said.' I would sooner send them to the West Indies as slaves.'

I walked down to the memorial to Sidney Gilchrist Thomas

Proud heyday: Blaenafon Workmen's Hall

who pioneered one of the great advances in steelmaking. By the 1870s the manufacture of steel had run into a seemingly insuperable problem. Ore containing phosphorus made poor steel. Sidney Gilchrist Thomas discovered a way of eliminating the phosphorus and found fame; but the fumes he inhaled during his experiments ruined his lungs and he died aged thirty-five.

John Evans, who has a passion for Blaenafon and its history, told me that it was once an exciting place. 'You could find entertainment every night of the week: theatres, circuses, fairs, visiting minstrels, parades and processions. It is hard to imagine it now but in the 1860s meetings were held to allocate weekends to the organisations which wanted to stage events – and there were not enough weekends in the year.'

The landscape around Blaenafon was thoroughly dug, hacked and tunnelled. To move their raw materials, engineers built a tunnel through the mountain, a mile and half long, from Blaenafon to Pwll-du, the longest tram tunnel in Britain. It is ripe for research and I came across an industrial archaeology group preparing to enter it, hoping to find abandoned equipment.

Today the Lamb and Fox and the village hall are the only surviving buildings in the village of Pwll-du, an oasis for travellers on the bare hilltop. In its time it was part of a hardworking coal community of several hundred people. Now Brian Lewis, the landlord, is the last link with the past. 'The king in my own little kingdom,' he smiled.

From the path of an old tramway, I had spectacular views of the Usk valley. Crickhowell lay to the west, Abergavenny to the east. In these hills Alexander Cordell set his novel *Rape of the Fair Country*, published in 1959, about the people whose lives were dominated by insatiable furnaces and greedy bosses. I passed what at first glance was a pile of rock, but historian Chris Barber told me it was slag from an ironworks. He showed me the remains of workshops and cottages.

'Three hundred people worked here, 1,300 feet up. It must have been a hell of a place. Iron ore was converted into wrought iron plates, rails and bars and taken by tramway around the mountain and down to the wharf at Llanfoist where it was loaded onto barges for shipment on the Brecknock and Abergavenny canal. It was cheaper than taking it down to Pontypool.'

Down the road on the site of the Queen Victoria pub, now demolished, I met Cyril Lewis. He told me about the night the pub

Rock and fire: site of the old Garnddyrys ironworks

floor collapsed. 'It was Easter Monday, everybody on holiday, the pub crowded with people singing and dancing. I was standing in the passage and heard this tremendous crash. The floor had gone and we were looking down at people in the hole. The piano was swaying on the edge. Luckily it didn't go down or it would have killed a few. But no-one was badly hurt; just cuts and bruises.'

Hang-gliders soared and swooped above me as I strode easily along the path curving around the Blorenge mountain. I turned into the forest on my left and walked the carpet of pine needles into the cathedral gloom. I had arranged a rendezvous with a group of archers and I walked with them as they sought out their targets. These were set up in the trees so that, rather as golfers go from hole to hole, the archers found their target, fired their arrows and walked to the next.

Paul Davis, their leader, thought the longbowmen who fought at Crecy and Agincourt would look down their noses at modern bows. 'We use bows developed in Victorian times with a draw-weight of 60lb for men, less for women. Medieval bows had a draw-weight between 80lb-150lb and I doubt there are many Welshmen today who could draw that sort of bow. But longbowmen in medieval times were yeomen and well-practised. And they must have had incredible physiques with shoulders like tallboys.' Such men, I supposed, were the ancestors of today's rugby forwards.

There was a slither here and there as I walked down the steep tree-shaded incline to Llanfoist. One hundred and fifty years ago the slope was a tramway noisy with the shouts of men and the rumble and shrieking of wagons heavy with coal, iron and limestone on their way to the canal wharf.

I ducked into the tunnel beneath the canal and emerged into a picture postcard scene. In its time this was the bustling junction where Blaenafon iron was loaded on barges for Newport for onward shipment to all the world's imagined corners. Now barges puttered sedately under the bridge, each one complete with bright paintwork, gleaming brass, chintz curtains, a dog and a contented skipper.

Llanfoist: memories of din

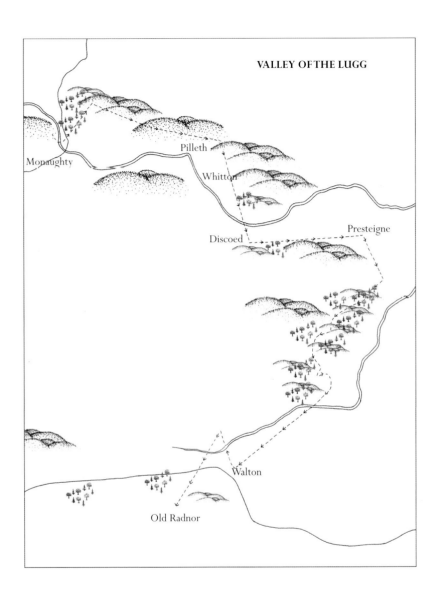

VALLEY OF THE LUGG

Monaughty

Pilleth

Whitton

Discoed

Presteigne

Walton

Old Radnor

4. VALLEY OF THE LUGG

Bells and the sparkling stream

Radnorshire has the feel of a private place, a little-known enclave on the border, an island set in the gentle hills. George Borrow, the traveller who strode the wild tracks of Wales in the 1850s, once asked a man in these parts for directions. 'Am I in England or Wales?' he wondered. 'Neither,' answered the man, 'you're in Radnorshire.'

Radnorshire: the lovely secret

I started my walk near the Elizabethan mansion called Monaughty, in its day the largest house in the county. James Price built it in 1565 to celebrate his marriage. His bride was a lady of the bedchamber to Queen Elizabeth. He spared no expense and hired the best craftsmen to create a house of great beauty. I found it thrilling and evocative. It calls upon the imagination to fill its dusty corridors and silent spacious rooms with the bustle, smells and laughter of a busy home. The house today is as it was more than four centuries ago. There is no electricity, no modern conveniences. To explore the house is to enter the past. I found in it an

Monaughty: a place for imagination

intimacy, rather than emptiness, as if its Elizabethan inhabitants slipped away only yesterday.

Douglas Blain, the owner, who showed me around, told me he had no intention of living in the house. 'I always wanted to restore it gently and put back the missing bits,' he said. 'I don't want to live in it because that would spoil it. I would have to live the life of a sixteenth-century gentleman which is not possible. I am a sort of anti-moderniser. However carefully you tried to modernise the house you would inevitably take something away. I am a connoisseur of atmosphere ... and the special atmosphere of the house is what we have done our best to preserve.'

Gentle restoration

The valley of the River Lugg winds through the hills towards Presteigne, among the woodlands where deciduous trees and conifers stand like armies toe to toe. I walked to the top of Black Hill and down to Pilleth. Here, in 1402, Owain Glyndwr won the greatest victory of his dozen years of fighting a war of independence against English rule. His courage and leadership at Pilleth, also known as the battle of Bryn Glas, established him as a Welsh hero, as a national figure rather than a guerrilla chief. Henry IV sent Edmund Mortimer here at the head of a strong army to smash Glyndwr's advance. But the arrows from the Welsh longbows fell like hail on Mortimer's men and there was terrible slaughter.

In *King Henry IV, Part I* Shakespeare tells of 'A post from Wales loaden with heavy news' – the defeat of Mortimer's troops by 'the irregular and wild Glendower'.

Mortimer was captured and later joined forces with his former enemy, marrying Glyndwr's daughter. In 1870 a ploughman unearthed a heap of bones, the mass grave of hundreds of men who died during the battle. A grove of pine trees was planted on the hillside above the church as a memorial.

Battlefield: a hail of arrows

I walked through Whitton and paused at the village school where generations of children were taught by the remarkable David Rhys Davies. He was headmaster at Whitton for half a century; but he was teaching long before that. He is in the record books as the longest-serving teacher in Britain. He taught until three days before his death in 1928 at the age of ninety-two, having logged seventy-six years in front of the blackboard.

The path led me south to Discoed, another handsome house of the sixteenth century, painstakingly restored by John Nethercott and his wife. They have established a business here, employing specialists to restore churches and old houses and furniture to their former glory.

Over the sparkling stream

In this twisty valley the Lugg achieves its ambition and becomes less a trickling stream and more a bolder river. Its odd blunt English name derives from a pretty one, the Welsh Llugwy, meaning a sparkling stream. It seemed that every other house had a story attached to it. Sadie Cole told me the story of Sarah Chandler, the farmer's wife at Dolley Farm in 1813, who was charged with forging banknotes and sentenced to death at Presteigne.

'But the night before the day of execution, her family broke into the jail, climbing a ladder over the wall. They removed steps from the front of the condemned cell and released their mother. She was found two years later, selling milk in Birmingham, and brought back to Presteigne. The death sentence was commuted and she was transported to New South Wales.'

Later she was joined by two of her sons. One was transported for shearing sheep and selling the fleeces; the other for stealing clothes from a line.

No doubt Sarah Chandler was helped to escape by the jailer and others. Perhaps the harshness of the judge was tempered by the compassion of the people. But Presteigne jail was hardly the Alcatraz of Wales. Many prisoners escaped, and one scrambled over the wall while heavily chained and minus his trousers.

Presteigne: good pull-in for judges

Pleasant Presteigne, Llanandras in Welsh, once prospered as a coaching town on the London to Aberystwyth road. I visited the most famous of its many agreeable buildings, the old Shire Hall, which was the court house and the Judge's Lodging. It was built between 1826 and 1829 on the site of the county jail and last used as a court in 1970. The building has been restored to its Victorian elegance and you can see why judges looked forward to a comfortable stretch in Presteigne. Indeed, the Lord Chief Justice himself declared these the best lodgings in England and Wales.

Upstairs there was every comfort and, below stairs, a large kitchen geared to healthy judicial appetites. Below that was the underworld, the labyrinth of the cells, used until 1900. When the pale and grubby prisoners were called to face trial it was only a few steps from the dark dungeon to the dock. When I climbed the stairs, emerging from the gloom of the cells and into the court, I could see why prisoners would have quailed.

The story is told of a local farmer sentenced to death in Presteigne. A few days later he stood on the scaffold nearby. A woman pushed through the tightly-packed crowd and called out. It was the farmer's wife and the hangman paused. She had one last poignant question to ask of her husband. 'Jack,' she cried, 'next year's potatoes – what field shall we plant them in?'

The handsome parish church of St Andrew, at the end of Broad Street, has been the witness of turbulent times, not least when Presteigne was disembowelled by Owain Glyndwr. In the handsome tower hang eight bells, cast in 1707, and when I climbed into the belfry they were in full swing. A team of Herefordshire bell ringers, commanded by the Reverend David Bowen, were spending the day travelling from church to church, ringing the bells. It is, apart from anything else, thoroughly good exercise, something noted by the eighteenth-century inventor of an exercise machine based on a church bell mechanism; and since it lacked the bell it was known as the dumb-bell.

Roy Stickling, the steeple keeper at St Andrew's, showed me the remarkable carillon, made in 1726. It plays every three hours, the church clock triggering its amazing mechanism of a drum, levers and a skein of wires. 'It's really an outsize musical box,' Roy said.

You can set your watch by Paul Preece. Each evening he arrives to ensure that Presteigne keeps faith with its history in the ceremony of the curfew bell. More than 430 years ago an Elizabethan

Tick, tock, the relentless clock harvests the minutes one by one

49

merchant founded a school in the town and insisted that the bell should be rung each evening until the end of time. Paul receives a fee to toll the knell of parting day. Much of it is paid by the musician Mike Oldfield who, when he lived in the district, composed his famous work *Tubular Bells*.

Mary's grave: casting stones

The church bells were perhaps the last sounds in the ears of poor Mary Morgan, just seventeen years old when she was hanged in 1805 for murdering her newborn daughter. She was condemned at Presteigne by Judge Hardinge, who had a reputation for imposing harsh sentences on women, and was very unpopular in the town.

Two stones stand over Mary's grave in the churchyard. The first, erected by a friend of Judge Hardinge, refers to him as 'benevolent' and in sanctimonious words blames Mary for her lack of Christian faith. The second reflects the feeling of people in the town who thought Mary's punishment too severe, and quotes the Christian message: 'He that is without sin among you let him first cast a stone at her.'

Nearby I found the grave of William Paytoe, governor of Presteigne jail in the years when many prisoners escaped. The verse on it reads: 'O silent grave to thee I trust – this precious pearl of worthy dust. And keep it safe O sacred tomb until a wife shall ask for room.'

Alas, no evidence exists that she ever joined him.

On my way out of Presteigne, I called on a man with a wonderful smile, Luigi Napolitano of Corton Farm. His life story is also a love story. He was taken prisoner during the Second World War and housed with other Italians in the POW camp near the farm. He worked on the land and was treated kindly by the farmer. As the months passed, he was attracted to the farmer's daughter, Betty, and when the war was over he married her in Pompeii. He returned to the farm and when Betty's father died he became the farmer. The buildings of the POW camp were demolished long ago; all except one, which Luigi has kept as a souvenir of his remarkable story.

'I am a lucky man,' he said. 'Betty's father was wonderful to me and I could not have wished for a better employer. Now Betty and I have two fine sons and five grandchildren. Who could want for better than that? My wish is that, in time, my ashes will lie here in the countryside where I have been so happy.'

One love story leads me to another. I took the path through the woods on the way to Walton. This is a landscape of little lanes and

Hindwell: a poet in love

quiet churchyards where the hillslopes gather strength and Wales begins to take on its rugged shape. I came to Hindwell and the handsome house where William Wordsworth and his wife Mary stayed. But they were never here together. William came in 1810, Mary in 1812. During their visits they sat by the lake and wrote to each other. The letters were discovered in a lawyer's office twelve years ago and are William and Mary's exquisite expressions of love, both for the countryside and for each other.

For Anne Goodwin, the farmer's wife, they are part of the romance of her home. 'There were 31 letters, beautifully written,' she said, and read me one of William's, which concluded: 'I am the blessedest of men.'

I passed the Four Stones, ancient glacial boulders standing like bulky rugby forwards, and marched on with the elegant hilltop church of Old Radnor in my sights.

On the upward path I walked over an archaeological site whose discovery has caused great excitement. A few years ago, a pilot flying over this land noticed hundreds of faint marks forming a gigantic circle. Investigation showed them to be post holes, the remnants of an immense prehistoric temple that makes Stonehenge look small.

Chris Martin, of Clwyd Powys Archaeological Trust, said the settlement was built five thousand years ago and its principal feature was a ring of 1,400 oak posts, each about 18 feet tall and each weighing four tons.

'It's a site of international significance,' he said, 'one of the largest and oldest circles of this kind ever found in Britain.'

Looking out from the slope at the broad sweep of the plain and its encircling hills I had the full measure of Radnorshire's beauty. I could understand why those people thousands of years ago chose it as their sacred place.

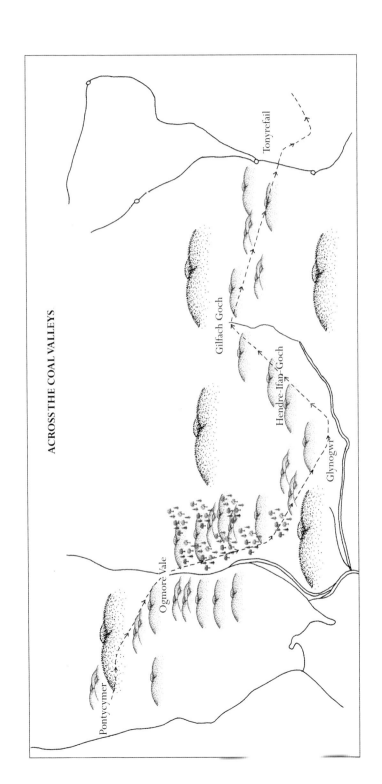

ACROSS THE COAL VALLEYS

Pontycymer

Ogmore Vale

Gilfach Goch

Hendre-Ifan-Goch

Glynogwr

Tonyrefail

5. ACROSS THE COAL VALLEYS

The clocks of different speeds

In the valleys of south Wales the names of collieries were once part of everyone's daily talk. Now they survive only in the reminiscences of grandfathers; and the mines themselves, extinct, covered-over and landscaped with grass and trees, are like legendary tombs.

I started this valley-hopping walk on the site of the Ffaldau colliery, on the edge of Pontycymer in the Garw Valley. It closed in 1985, a footnote in the familiar story of the dwindling of coal and community. In a few minutes I was sitting in a room on the main street, listening to a dozen or so men, many of them former miners, who were the witnesses of an age and a way of life that vanished so suddenly. They belong to a discussion group and meet every Tuesday to talk over old times and keep their history alive.

'In years to come people will find it hard to believe how men worked underground,' they said. 'Working on your knees ...'

'... and the rats, so many rats, I was petrified of them.'

Pontycymer: Houdini escaped

'You depended so much on your mates you couldn't afford to have an enemy underground.'

'But I remember the jazz bands and festivals, too, all the entertainments that compensated for the horrors.'

People in Pontycymer used to turn out in force to see the shows at the old Hippodrome music hall. For years it was run by the show business family Anderson: Harry, the acrobat, his wife Amy, who would throw bananas to the audience, and her sister Harriet, a male impersonator. Grafton Radcliffe, who saw one of their shows, told me that, as a favour to the Andersons, stars like Charlie Chaplin, Houdini, Stan Laurel, Lillie Langtry and George Robey appeared at the Hippodrome. It was the show business capital of the valleys.

'But in 1922 it burnt down and the Andersons were left destitute,' said Grafton. 'They had only intended staying a few years in Pontycymer, but they were stranded here for the rest of their lives. To make ends meet, Harry became a miner and Harriet sold paraffin from a horse and cart. Still, they continued to put on shows and thanks to their West End contacts they dressed in wonderful costumes.'

In a few minutes I was striding the mountain path out of Pontycymer. Even halfway up, I had a good view of the Garw. Before

Over the top: the stride to Ogmore Vale

Streetscape

the collieries only 78 people lived in the entire valley and the only sound to be heard up here was of the huntsman and his hounds and the shepherd and his sheep.

A half-hour push brought me to the naked saddle of the mountain and I had an easy and exhilarating swoop into Ogmore Vale. I had arranged to meet John Courts at his pigeon loft. In common with many former mining men he was gripped by a passion for racing his pigeons. As we sat and waited for his birds to come home he explained to me the joy of owning them, the freedom, grace and beauty they embody, the thrill and pride he feels as they

Valleys beauties...
pampered pigeon

...and cossetted chrysanth

come into sight after navigating hundreds of miles across Europe. Although he has raced them for years he still marvels at the mystery of natural navigation. He pointed with unconcealed excitement as half a dozen birds appeared above the mountain, wheeled around his home and, one by one, fluttered into the loft.

'It's a beautiful moment when a bird come home after a long flight. Your heart is shaking.'

Another sort of beauty lies at the heart of that other valleys passion, chrysanthemums. Tony Cannon showed me the blooms he was preparing for a show. 'I'm up early in the morning and with them late into the night.' On the big day the flowers are groomed and glossed, tweaked and titivated, crimped and primped like Saturday brides.

From Ogmore Vale I walked over the mountain into the Dimbath Valley. No coal was ever found here and it appears as much of south Wales used to look, before woodcutters felled the forests and builders came to stitch terraces to the hillsides.

In the churchyard at Glynogwr I found a clump of splendid Pyrenean lilies, exotic immigrants far from home, thriving in the upland air. My particular interest in the church was the effigy near

Medieval wild tracks: pilgrim's progress

the altar. This was of a great walker, a medieval pilgrim, display-
ing the adornments which indicate where his faith took him. Keys,
crosses and shells show that he went to Rome, Jerusalem and to
Santiago de Compostela in Spain.

More than 1,400 years ago, the pioneering Celtic saint Tyfodwg
founded a church on this land and monks set out to spread the
word. They trekked over the surrounding hills and I followed in
their footsteps towards the next valley with small farms as my land-
marks.

At Hendre-Ifan-Goch I was shown the old two-seater ty bach,
a monument to a more companionable age. The farm was owned
in the eighteenth century by Lewis Hopkin, stonemason, carpenter, modest poet and a literary leader in Glamorgan who taught,
among others, the poet Iolo Morganwg.

Hendre-Ifan-Goch: literary flowering

Betsi Griffiths, an admirer of Lewis Hopkin, told me about his
two dwarf children, one of whom was the celebrated Hopkin
Hopkin. 'He was only 32 inches tall and his parents once took him
to Bristol where people paid to see him. He also went to London
and met the future King George III.' The suit that Hopkin Hopkin
wore to meet the king is preserved in the Museum of Welsh Life
in St Fagans. Poor Hopkin: he died of old age when he was only
eighteen.

Gilfach Goch: coal and stories

I walked down into Gilfach Goch. The first pit here was sunk in 1862 and within twenty years the district was booming. Some of the valley's story forms the background to Richard Llewellyn's novel *How Green Was My Valley*, published in 1939. Like the Hollywood film based upon it the story is much more myth than history; and to people in the valleys it bore little resemblance to the hard lives they led. Its very success nevertheless made it a part of the saga of coal. Richard Llewellyn earned his fortune from it. He claimed to have worked as a miner, though he never had any first-hand experience of labouring underground. Rather, he listened to miners and to his aunt and uncle whom he visited in Gilfach. And he used his imagination.

Teifion Griffiths told me that Llewellyn visited Gilfach Goch in the 1930s. 'He came here with my uncle, Will Griffiths, and visited my grandfather who told him stories of how the valley developed. My grandfather came in the 1870s from Merthyr and was one of the earliest Gilfach settlers.' Teifion showed me the first edition of *How Green Was My Valley* that Llewellyn gave to his grandfather and inscribed: 'To Joseph Griffiths of Gilfach Goch whom I am proud to call my friend.'

Several pubs played their part in Gilfach's rumbustious heyday. The Ogmore was kept for years by the formidable Mrs Jennie

Jones who not only pulled pints but played the church organ and rode to hounds. One night she was awakened by a prowler. She took a pistol from her drawer and fearlessly opened the door shouting: 'Give yourself up or I fire.' Then she heard the all too recognizable voice of one of her regulars. 'Don't shoot, Mrs Jones bach ... it's only me stealing your coal.'

During the First World War Mrs Jones persuaded the authorities that Gilfach miners would dig more coal if they had more beer. Hearing this wonderful news men from neighbouring valleys came over the mountain bringing their own glasses.

In the ruins of the Six Bells, Ruth James told me of the years when it was run by her parents. 'It was always lively and provided plenty of entertainment. Boxing matches were staged in a large room upstairs.'

They were certainly better-regulated boxing bouts than those I heard about from Johnny Jones. At remote spots in the mountains, away from the eyes of the police, bare-knuckle fighters slugged each other with ruthless savagery while yelling spectators laid their bets. 'A match would be arranged between the hard man from Gilfach who would fight the hard man from, say, Tonypandy. The word was passed from mouth to mouth and a huge crowd would gather. The men fought until they dropped.'

Gilfach Goch was the first valley in Wales to be restored at the end of the mining epoch. In the early 1970s, after 110 years of mining, the removal of three million tons of waste and the reshaping of the land enabled people to see across the valley once again.

Crossing the top of the hill, walking towards Tonyrefail, I enjoyed a grand panorama of valleys, the Ely, the Rhondda, the Taff and, in the blue distance, the hills of Rhymney. I passed by Cae'r-lan, a farmhouse rebuilt by Lewis Hopkin. He it was who carved the sundial above the front door, revealing his Latin learning with the inscription *tempus irreparibile fugit* ... time flies and you can't get it back.

The hillsides around here are riddled with old coal workings, mostly forgotten now. I came across the stone archway of a flooded mine and saw that nature had reclaimed everything in the vicinity. Wetland plants flourished and I noted some spotted orchid, ragged robin, greater spearwort, forget-me-not, cuckoo flower and knapweed.

An unlikely spot, a car park in Tonyrefail, yielded a surprising story. In a corner were some old memorial stones ... and one of

Latin scholarship: Lewis Hopkin's time at Cae'r-lan

them was a murder stone. It was a custom in parts of Wales, when a murderer had not been brought to justice, to record that fact on the victim's tombstone and to add, in elaborate words, that in this world or the next the guilty will be punished.

The stone in Tonyrefail recorded the killing of Jane Lewis, a farm servant of twenty-three, in December 1862. She had been murdered 'by a cruel hand and tho her blood is hitherto unavenged attention is directed to the day when light will have shone on the

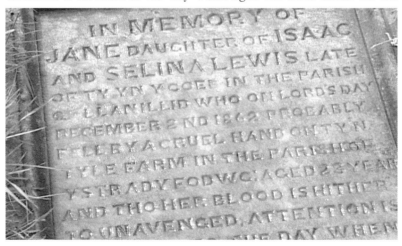

Murder stone: Jane Lewis and a cruel hand

mysterious occurrence and guilt be accorded its just reward ... God lives – revenge is His'.

Jane was stabbed to death one Sunday as she walked from chapel through the woods to her home at Tyntyla Farm. The murder shocked all of Wales and is still remembered. The story was turned into a play.

I heard more from David and Joyce Rees who farm at Tylcha Ganol near Tonyrefail. They gave me tea and cake and told me all about it. The story had come down through their family from Granny Tyntyla who knew Jane and told her children and grand-children. David and Joyce said that Jane had two admirers and may have been a victim of jealousy. She was murdered in the woods with a cut-throat razor kept on top of a long-case clock at Tyntyla. Today that clock in the Rees's farm is still ticking away.

'The murderer was never found,' Joyce said, 'but an intriguing part of the story is that many years later, in Australia, an old man confessed to killing Jane.'

Like a number of the people farming these hillsides, the Reeses are part of a social continuity. They showed me the names inked into their great family bible. 'I am the fourth generation to farm here,' David said. 'We were here before coal, we saw coal come and go.'

In the bible: the family story

Amidst all the turmoil of coal, cheek by jowl with the most intensively mined district of the world, these farming families maintained their own way of life, a world apart. It is as if the clocks ticked at different speeds, the urgent pace of industry and the measured rhythm of the land.

I walked the road to the dramatically-named Pant-y-brad, the dell of treachery. Walter Jones, a local historian, told me that the site was a good example of the mingling of history and myth. A marble slab put here in 1909 notes that on November 16 1326 King Edward II, the first English Prince of Wales, was taken prisoner here.

'There is little evidence that he was captured at this spot,' Walter said, 'but he was certainly captured in south Wales during the war between himself and his queen, Isabella. He was taken to Llantrisant Castle and then to Berkeley Castle in Gloucestershire where he was put to death.'

Treachery: the King's road to doom

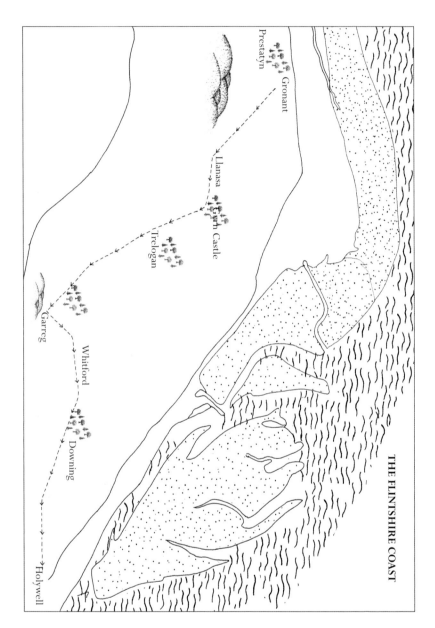

THE FLINTSHIRE COAST

Prestatyn

Gronant

Llanasa

Gwth Castle

Trelogan

Garreg

Whitford

Downing

Holywell

6. THE FLINTSHIRE COAST

Water and wine

Below me, as I climbed the hill above Gronant, the sea waged its endless war of attrition against the dunes. Beyond the eighteenth-century lighthouse on the sandy Point of Ayr, across the Welsh Channel and the Wild Road and the broad mouth of the River Dee, I made out the distant docks of Liverpool. From these northern hillsides Flintshire has always kept an eye upon the sea.

I soon reached the old Voel Nant telegraph house, one of the chain of 12 semaphore stations built across north Wales from Liverpool to Holyhead to transmit news of ships sailing into and out of Liverpool.

The original telegraph was built in 1826 and working by 1827 when the arrival of an American ship, the *Napoleon*, was reported. The line was improved in 1841 when the new station was constructed at Voel Nant.

A newspaper once proclaimed that messages could travel 'faster than the wind' and it was often said that a signal could reach Holyhead from Liverpool in under half a minute, but there is no evidence for this. It was much more likely that even in clear weather it took a minute or more for the operators in each station to note a signal and pass it on to the next relay. Still, a signal from

On message: telegraph station at Voel Nant

An eye on the sea: Point of Ayr and hazy Mersey

Holyhead to Liverpool in about 15 minutes was excitingly rapid and a boon to shipowners. I imagined them looking at the messages telling them that their ships, which had voyaged from the earth's ends, had been sighted off Anglesey. I saw them rubbing their hands in the expectation that rich cargoes would soon be unloaded. The semaphore was replaced by the electric telegraph in 1861.

This part of the country was dominated for centuries by the Mostyns, one of the great dynastic families of Wales. One of them, Richard ap Howel, famously supported Henry VII in his struggle to win the throne from Richard III and fought for him in the decisive battle at Bosworth in 1485. The family were notable patrons of poets and in the seventeenth century, in Mostyn Hall, amassed one of the outstanding country house libraries of Wales.

To my left, as I walked the hillside, I saw Talacre Abbey, half hidden in the woods, a vast Gothic pile that made me think of a scary Hollywood melodrama. The Catholic branch of the Mostyns built it in the 1820s but, a century later, crippled by taxes, sold it as a retreat to an order of nuns. This sisterhood added a simple church in 1932 and built a high wall to enclose their sanctuary. But, like the Mostyns before them, they found the mansion too costly to run and moved away.

A chilling story is told about the Talacre estate. Some of the

Talacre: death and taxes...

... and the sanctuary of the nuns

Talacre Mostyns believe their family was cursed by a witch for selling the family land. Certainly Sir Pyers Mostyn, who sold it, was killed in a plane crash in Kenya; and his son was killed, also in Kenya, by a mad horse. Two of his successors died young and it is said that the curse will only be lifted when the Mostyns return to Talacre.

I paused for a while in Llanasa, snug in its valley and as neat and brushed as a schoolgirl on the first day of term, a prizewinner for its appearance and its embroidery of flowerbeds.

It was a short walk up to Gyrn Castle, which commands the hilltop. Sir Geoffrey Bates, its owner, is the great-grandson of the Victorian shipowner Sir Edward Bates who lived here for some years. Sir Edward owned a fleet of vessels, many of them in the India trade, carrying spices and textiles to Britain. Genial Sir Geoffrey showed me the old man's formidable brass telescope, which seemed to me as big as an anti-aircraft gun, mounted on a tripod. 'He used this to keep a lookout for his ships as they made their way to Liverpool. When he spotted one he hurried down to Mostyn where he kept a steam yacht and set off to meet her.'

With his fortune made from shipping, Sir Edward became a Member of Parliament. Three of his grandsons became chairmen

Gyrn Castle: when my ship comes in

of the Cunard shipping line. Another descendant, Frederick Bates, was a naturalist and pioneer film maker. In the woodlands of the Gyrn estate he set up his camera in a hide to film badgers, otters and foxes.

'He set up lamps to film the badgers at night,' Sir Geoffrey said, 'and turned up the brightness very gradually so that they did not become alarmed.' Some of the footage survives: scenes of foxes and cubs, otters playing in the streams and badgers emerging cautiously from their setts.

The footpath took me through a meadow brilliant with buttercups into Trelogan. It is a small village, overlooked by many guides, but it has three features worth a boast. Emlyn Williams, the playwright and actor, was a pupil in the village school before the First World War. Close by is the home of David Lloyd, the tenor hugely popular in Wales, a master of Mozart and Verdi, and an inspiration during the Second World War. Born in 1912, the son of a miner, he had a humble start and was a carpenter's apprentice at fourteen before his talent was discovered. He died in 1969 but, as I saw, his sisters keep the parlour as it was when he was a star.

The name of Trelogan is also famous throughout the scientific world. Goronwy Wynne, a botanist, told me why. Since ancient times Flintshire earned part of its living from mining lead and zinc. Centuries of lead mining at Trelogan left a remarkable legacy. A few acres were used as a dump for lead mine waste and became horribly poisoned. Yet certain plants, grasses and flowers began to adapt and to flourish. They migrated from the nearby pastures and in the space of two hundred years became metal-tolerant. They gradually evolved as survivors, slow-growing plants, different in shape from their pasture neighbours, with an ability to prosper on polluted soil, needing little nutrient and resistant to drought.

'Trelogan grasses have been grown commercially and are used world-wide,' Goronwy said. 'In the United States, Australia and the Far East scientists know of Trelogan ... the place where pioneering work has been done on lead-tolerant plants and where we have learnt much about evolution.'

I trekked south-east and took in a wonderful panorama: Point of Ayr, the Wirral and Hilbre Island sea bird sanctuary. In the distance the faint smudge of Blackpool Tower rose from the candyfloss mist.

Crossing a field I paid my respects to a stone, Maen Achwyfan,

Maen Achwyfan, the thousand year landmark

that has stood like a sentry for a thousand years or more. It is 12 feet high and intricately carved with Viking-influenced Celtic designs. I sometimes think, looking at these mysterious ancient stones in Wales, that when men land on the plains of Mars they will find one waiting for them.

On the top of Garreg Mountain I looked into the stubby thumb of the stone tower that many scholars believed was built by the Romans as a lighthouse. In fact it was constructed about four hundred years ago as a beacon to warn the countryside that pirate ships from Ireland or the Isle of Man were on their way; and it was restored in 1897 to salute Queen Victoria's diamond jubilee.

Not far from Whitford I called on Gaynor Bailey, a leading breeder and trainer of gun dogs, and spent an entertaining and instructive hour watching her teach her young pupils. It was particularly enjoyable because the dogs enjoyed it, too; and they were all perfectly behaved.

The handsome nineteenth-century church is the outstanding feature of Whitford. Tudor Williams, the verger here for more than thirty years, told me of the pleasure he derives from serving the church and being part of its rhythm and continuity. He sets the stage for baptisms, weddings and funerals and I watched him at his familiar tasks, cleaning the brasswork, trimming the churchyard grass and ringing the bells. 'I never miss a day,' he said. 'My father

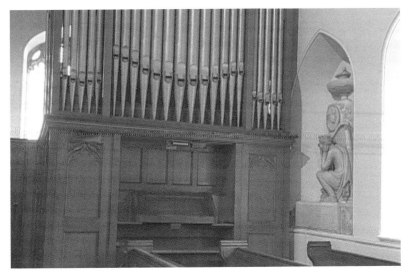

Pennant remembered in Whitford church

was verger for forty-one years. Maybe it is in the blood.'

Near the organ is a fine monument to Thomas Pennant, the naturalist and traveller. He roamed widely in Ireland, Scotland and Wales, and his travel writing was admired by Dr Johnson. His two-volume *Tours in Wales*, 1778 and 1781, illustrated by Moses Griffiths, was a pioneering work. Griffiths is buried in the churchyard and when his grave was 'lost' some years ago, Tudor Williams searched for it and found it against a wall, concealed by ivy.

Paul Evans, who has made a detailed study of Pennant's work, told me: 'In his time he was a gifted observer and was once described as Britain's greatest zoologist before Darwin. I would like more people to appreciate his achievements. He is a rather neglected figure these days.'

Although a devoted rover, Pennant always returned to his beloved base, the house near Whitford called Downing, where he was born, lived and died. The house was destroyed by fire in 1922 and nothing remains of it. Pennant was a friend of the naturalist Joseph Banks who sailed with Captain Cook on the first of his three great Pacific voyages, from 1768 to1771. During their many long conversations Banks told Cook a lot about his friend, how they used to make botany and geology expeditions in Wales. When Cook discovered and charted the east coast of Australia the question of a name arose. There was already a New England, a new

Scotland (Nova Scotia) and a New Ireland. Cook called it New Wales; and Banks knew how much that would please Pennant. In 1840 the southern part of this vast stretch of land was designated New South Wales, but the northern part was not called New North Wales. Instead it became Queensland.

Climbing a stile, I emerged from the woods near Downing onto a well-barbered golf course. The clear footpath ensured that golfers and walkers could enjoy a civilised co-existence.

I walked down into Holywell along streets well-worn by pilgrims' feet. The abundant waters of the well were a source of wonder in pagan times and gradually became absorbed into Christian traditions. For many centuries this place has been one of the great shrines of Britain, drawing a constant traffic of pilgrims. Four kings have journeyed here for blessing. The chapel was built five hundred years ago by Margaret Beaufort, the mother of Henry VII. In particular, the well has a special significance for Catholics. It is dedicated to St Winifred, who, in the story that evolved in the seventh century, was beheaded by a would-be seducer angered by her robust defence of her virginity. The gush of her blood became the healing stream of the well. Her uncle, St Beuno, restored her head to her body. As honoured as Lourdes, St Winifred's well has

Holywell: the power of healing

Holywell and an old story

long been a place of hope for the sick and disabled. The stone canopy over the water is scratched and cut with the names of grateful pilgrims.

I stood beside the entrance to watch scores of people take part in the annual procession of Catholics, walking down the hill to pay homage to St Winifred. On the pavement a handful of fundamentalist Protestants stood to jeer them and wave placards, an echo of old divisions and old prejudices that shaped our history; yet an alien spectacle in modern Wales.

It was discovered long ago that because the parish church stands in a hollow the sound of the steeple bell could not be heard in the town above. The answer was to employ a man, known as the walking steeple, to walk through the streets ringing a bell. He hung it by a strap around his neck and banged it against a leather pad buckled to his thigh. Thus the steeple went to the people.

In a storeroom by the well I was shown ten religious banners painted for the local Catholic church a century ago by an obsessed and bitter man, Frederick William Rolfe, who lived in Holywell from 1895 to 1898. As payment for the paintings he was given food and shelter by the local priest. Rolfe was a writer and in 1904

Paintings by Corvo, the bitter Baron

he published a novel, *Hadrian the Seventh*, about a penurious author who became Pope. Rolfe himself longed to be a Roman Catholic priest.

David Schwarz told me some of his story. 'He came out of a seminary – some say he was thrown out – and for a time edited a local paper, *The Holywell Record*. But his editorials were so scurrilous that people refused to buy the paper and it went bankrupt.'

Rolfe had a notoriously acrid temper and he abused his friends as much as he sponged on them. He tried several times to become a priest and failed, although he called himself Father Rolfe all the same. Such were his delusions of grandeur that when he went to live in Italy he awarded himself the title of Baron Corvo. He died in Venice in 1913, penniless.

The flow of the spring water in Holywell is today much reduced. But for centuries there was a mighty torrent, the greatest and most powerful spring in Britain. This benefited the town in two ways, by attracting pilgrims and tourists and by providing industrialists with a source of power to turn their wheels, 25,000 gallons a minute. The water powered the valley's industries, cotton and paper factories, and was stored in huge mill ponds. Above all, the water powered the mills that rolled out an endless ribbon of shining copper. These were run by Thomas Williams, known as the Copper King, an Anglesey lawyer who became the most powerful British businessman of the eighteenth century.

'He made his fortune from the copper sheets nailed to the bottoms of ships to protect them from marine growths and the worms that bored holes in the hulls,' Ken Davies told me. 'He also developed copper bolts to keep the sheets in place.' Thomas Williams's copper helped to keep the Royal Navy at sea in the long and dangerous years of the Napoleonic wars.

I ended the walk in evening sunshine which turned the stones of Basingwerk Abbey into gold. The monks here were the first to use the power of the Holywell stream. It drove the mills where they ground their corn. After the monks were driven out during Henry VIII's Dissolution of the Monasteries the abbey stones were used in the construction of factories.

But long before that the monks were famous for their hospitality. Pilgrims would travel to Holywell to take the waters, and move on to Basingwerk to take the wines. To accompany dinner, and to go with their blessings, the monks offered a choice of French and Spanish vintages.

Basingwerk: bread and wine

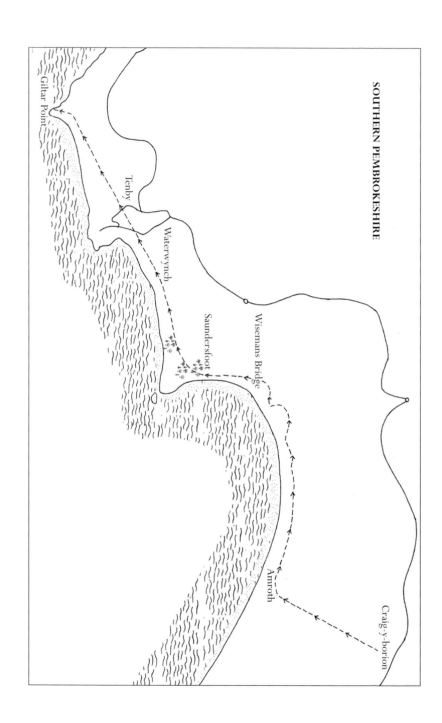

SOUTHERN PEMBROKESHIRE

Giltar Point

Tenby

Waterwynch

Saundersfoot

Wisemans Bridge

Amroth

Craig-y-borion

7. SOUTHERN PEMBROKESHIRE

A journey to the genius rock

Craig-y-borion was the home in the 1850s of Mr and Mrs Severn. Mr Severn pursued a passionate affair with a pretty governess and, in a severe case of Victorian self-righteousness, some local people seized him and stuck him on a ceffyl pren, a wooden horse. This was a traditional way of shaming those who broke the moral code. As it happened, it was the last time the ceffyl pren was used in the district. These days the Sunday newspapers do the job. Did Mr Severn slink back to his wife in disgrace? No. He ran off with the governess.

I started at Craig-y-borion, heading for Amroth and planning to follow the coastal path to Tenby and out to Giltar Point where there is a magnificent view of Caldy Island. I wandered through a wooded valley to Colby Lodge, a National Trust house with a lovely walled garden and a gazebo painted with numerous *trompe l'œil* images.

Colby: peak of the gardener's art

Back on the path, among the buttercups, I found the opening of an old mine, a reminder that Pembrokeshire once had rich reserves of iron ore and anthracite. Queen Victoria insisted that

Baby Pit: Victorian tragedy and redemption

only Pembrokeshire anthracite would do for the stove in her royal yacht. According to a mines inspector in the 1840s, women in the Pembrokeshire pits 'worked harder than slaves in the West Indies'.

Quite soon, I came to a circle of laurel marking an old mine shaft known as the Baby Pit. 'A distraught young woman, Mary Prout, threw her month-old illegitimate child into it and was convicted of murder,' Roscoe Howells, the writer and historian, told me. 'That was in 1864. The death sentence was commuted to twenty years' imprisonment. When Mary was freed, she married a local man, lived happily and won back her respectability.' Roscoe showed me her gravestone in Amroth churchyard with an inscription composed by her adoring children.

He also took me to the beach to show me the cliffs. 'Those aren't sea caves,' he said, pointing out the holes in the cliffs. 'They were made by men digging out the iron ore, thousands of tons of it. It was picked over by women, known as pollers, and then taken away in open boats.'

During 1943, on the curve of Carmarthen Bay from Pendine to Saundersfoot, there was a full-scale rehearsal for the D-Day landings that in 1944 would liberate Europe. The beaches resemble those of Normandy. Thousands of men came ashore in landing craft and valuable lessons were learnt. Even though the operation was on an enormous scale it was kept secret. The entire coast was put under curfew for 16 days. Cameras and binoculars were banned and mail censored. Nothing leaked out.

Olive Cooke, whose parents ran the Wisemans Bridge Hotel, told me of the excitement of all the military bustle, the ships and the fighting men, and the cavalcade of cars carrying the Allied top brass who came to witness the rehearsal. She took trays of tea to Prime Minister Winston Churchill and General Eisenhower.

I walked beside the beach and then through the old railway tunnels into Saundersfoot. The tunnels were once used by trains carrying anthracite to Saundersfoot; but looking at the harbour on a sunny morning, with its pretty cottages and yachts and flotillas of dinghies, it was hard to imagine that it was once a workaday coal port. I passed the house built for the family of Joan Hunter Dunn, the girl who inspired the longings of John Betjeman who, in *A Subaltern's Love-song*, wrote famously of '... Miss J. Hunter Dunn/Furnish'd and burnish'd by Aldershot sun.'

Climbing out of Saundersfoot I paused at the hillside meadow where William Frost, a local carpenter and chapel deacon, supposedly took to the air in his home-made flying machine. This was in 1896, seven years before the Wright brothers made their historic flight in North Carolina. Some spindly drawings on a patent docu-

Nº 20,431  A.D. 1894

Date of Application, 25th Oct. 1894
Complete Specification Left, 25th July, 1895—Accepted, 19th Oct., 1895

PROVISIONAL SPECIFICATION.

A Flying Machine.

WILLIAM FROST Carpenter and Builder Saundersfoot Pembrokeshire do hereby declare the nature of this invention to be as follows :—

The flying machine is propelled into the air by two reversible fans revolving horizontally. When sufficient height is gained, wings are spread and tilted by 5 means of a lever, causing the machine to float onward and downward. When low enough the lever is reversed causing it to rise upward & onward. When required to stop it the wings are tilted so as to hold against the wind or air and lowered by the reversible fans. The steering is done by a helm fitted to front of machine.

October 25th 1894.

10   WILLIAM FROST.

Flight, or flight of fancy

ment of 1894 depict a sort of hydrogen balloon with the pilot sitting in a wire basket beneath it, turning a hand-cranked propeller. When he tried to get development money from the government, William Frost was told that there was no intention of using flying machines in war.

Whether he really did get off the ground remains a matter of argument. There was no photograph of the machine or any reliable independent eyewitness of a flight. Some loyal local people believe William Frost's story that the contraption actually took to the air and flew 500 yards or more before hitting a tree. But, even if true, it was hardly a powered flight. Paul Williams, an engineer who has studied the design, told me that it was doubtful that the machine flew. 'My engineering heart,' he said regretfully, 'says no.'

Walking south along the beach I passed the striking geological formation, known as the Ladies Cave, but properly called an anticline. It was a popular attraction for Victorians and starred in the picture postcards they sent to their friends. High on the cliff I followed the path towards Tenby and, as I rounded a bend, the town came into view, as if a curtain had lifted on a theatre set. It was painted by a soft pastel light and looked like a province of the Mediterranean transported as a gift to Wales.

I walked the beach past Waterwynch, the home of Charles

Coasting along to Tenby

A town with tales to tell

Norris who had two passions in his life. The first was the pretty girl who caught his eye as he rode with his regiment through Coventry. He eloped with her. The second was Tenby. He sailed his yacht into the harbour in 1805 and was at once smitten by the town. Indeed, he stayed for the rest of his life and made numerous sketches and paintings of it. His legacy includes more than 1,200 drawings of the sea, the ships and Tenby itself. In those days part of the town was still in ruins after the Civil War.

The beach forms a grand avenue into the heart of Tenby, known in Welsh as Dinbych-y-Pysgod, Tenby of the Fishes. Countless children have spent summer holidays on these sands and learnt the meaning of the word bliss. The rock pools are home to exotic starfish and to the famous Tenby prawns. You can catch fresh prawns for supper if you know where to look.

When people hear the name of the magnate Sir William Paxton they often think of the ludicrous tower he built near Carmarthen to prove he still had plenty of money after buying 25,000 gallons of beer, 11,000 bottles of whisky and 8,000 bottles of port to bribe the voters in an election, which he lost. But Tenby itself is a better monument to his taste and fortune. He gave Tenby a water supply and built the Georgian houses, a theatre and spa, all of which made the town a handsome, fashionable and famous resort. His bath

Fashionable, famous and clean behind the ears

Notice. These Rocks & Beach are reserved for the exclusive use of Ladies and Children after 10 o'clock in the morning. Gentlemen are requested to abstain from bathing at this place after the above hour.
By Order:
Richard Hare, Agent.
Heam Castle,
Aug.st 30th 1880.
Henry Thomas, Harbour Master.

Gentlemen took the early bath

house still bears the inscription in Greek: the sea cleanses all man's pollution. Today we know that, unfortunately, it does not.

From the very early days Tenby was in the swim. For many years women taking the health cure of sea bathing put themselves in the hands of Peggy Davies, the bathing woman, who for forty-two years grasped her clients and dunked them under the waves. A memorial tablet to Peggy records that her clients were truly grateful for her good-humoured services. Fittingly, the dunker herself died in the sea of a heart attack in 1809.

No rules prevailed in the early years of sea bathing. As John Tipton, the former curator of the town's fascinating museum, explained, people simply took off their clothes and ran into the sea.

But in Victorian times sea bathing raised ticklish questions of modesty. In the seaside garden of Eden, how did you stop Adam peeping at Eve? Rules were introduced and, as the Victorian age became ever more Victorian, Tenby was in the forefront of bathing decorum. Photographs show the beach crowded with the wheeled bathing machines that delivered well-covered swimmers to the water's edge.

No man, said John Tipton, could step from a bathing machine less than 60 yards from a machine used by a woman. 'Men had to row out 200 yards and not approach within 100 yards of a beach where ladies were swimming. There was disapproval of the men who stood on Castle Hill and looked at the ladies popping out of the bathing machines below. These regulations were still in force in 1914, but from the turn of the century people had started bathing more freely.'

Tenby was a busy port and boom town in Tudor times and the Tudor Merchant's House in Bridge Street provides a window into the good life lived here five hundred years ago by a man of substance and fashion. The merchant and his family enjoyed the very latest foreign imports of spices and wine. We are well-informed about their diet because the remains of what they ate have been preserved in the midden below the latrine which was next to the kitchen. Ken Murphy, of Cambria Archaeology, who spent a summer digging in the midden, listed what had been found: the seeds of North African figs, the pips of French grapes, the bones of mackerel and finches, partridges and rabbits. And the first oranges to reach Wales were landed in Tenby.

'The people in this house had a good diet,' Ken Murphy said, 'and it is only in the past twenty or thirty years that most people have achieved that sort of quality. But we also know that worm infestations were common and that people were troubled by rats.'

Boots The Chemists, in the town centre, allowed me to see the secret tunnel that lies beyond their storeroom beneath the shop. Ruth Foster guided me through the narrow passage into a small and chilly room. At one time, it is thought, a tunnel led from this room to St Mary's church across the road and another went down to the harbour. In the dangerous aftermath of the battle of Tewkesbury in 1471 young Henry Tudor fled to Tenby with his uncle Jasper. The Mayor of Tenby helped them escape. They made their way through the tunnels beneath the town and, the story goes, waited in the secret room until the coast was clear. They were smuggled aboard a ship for France. A year later Henry Tudor returned, landed in Wales, gathered support and eventually took the throne as Henry VII.

Taking the Underground to power

St Mary's is a wonderful medieval church with a wealth of fine carving. It has a memorial to Robert Recorde, the Tenby-born mathematician who invented the plus, minus and equals signs. It also has a souvenir of the sieges of the Civil War when it was twice taken by Cromwell's forces and twice bombarded from the sea.

Cromwellian troops stormed into the church and, in the gloom, one of them mistook a kneeling figure of a Mayor of Tenby for a Cavalier soldier. As we can see to this day the jittery Roundhead raised his musket and shot the mayoral nose to smithereens.

A mural in the market hall tells Tenby's story. There's Henry Tudor on the run, Nelson visiting in 1802, the Tenby daffodil, once almost extinct and now re-established, the Tenby blitz – a single German bomb – and a thriller by Dick Francis, reminding us that he springs from the time when Tenby was a horse-racing town.

The jewels of Tenby

The mural also features the Tenby beetle stones, large pebbles found on the shore. When cut they reveal an exotic design which can look like a beetle. Hedley Smith is the last of the enthusiasts. He knows where to find the stones and how to cut and polish them. He gives them to his friends.

'Years ago they were much sought after and sold in Tenby jewellers' shops. I remember seeing them in the windows, beautiful and gleaming in the sun.'

To squeeze a little more from the day I headed across the South Beach to climb the winding path up the outcrop of Giltar Point. In the late afternoon light Tenby seemed burnished. I sat and contemplated Caldey, a Christian settlement since the sixth century, where the monks cultivate lavender and broom to make their lovely perfumes and add a fragrance to their prayers.

Giltar Point was a favourite swimming place for Augustus John, the portrait painter born in Tenby in 1878. One day he dived into the sea here and cracked his head on a rock and bled copiously. After that he seemed to change. Out of the incident grew one of the legends of Augustus John. Summarised on the back of a Brooke Bond Tea card in a series of famous people, it said that he hit his head on a rock 'and emerged from the water a genius'.

Giltar: the artist's leap

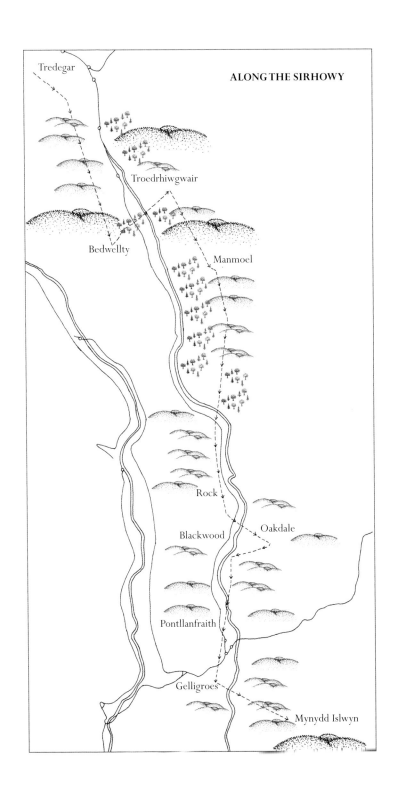

ALONG THE SIRHOWY

Tredegar

Troedrhiwgwair

Bedwellty

Manmoel

Rock

Blackwood

Oakdale

Pontllanfraith

Gelligroes

Mynydd Islwyn

8. ALONG THE SIRHOWY

A place of revolution

Tredegar is one of those words that encapsulates a whole history. The people who poured in to dig coal and work iron in this company town fashioned a remarkable society. It was alive with the political ideas of angry and vigorous young men and women impatient for change. Its spirit was articulated most famously by the rebellious young miner Aneurin Bevan who, like many others, absorbed the books in the Workmen's Library and forged an astonishing eloquence to match his principles and emotions.

I started on the edge of town, 1,200 feet up at Parc Bryn Bach. Here on the very fringe of the Brecon Beacons there were once the coal mine and iron ore patches that gave birth to Tredegar. Now the scars are covered by a lake and a landscaped park. Following the Sirhowy river I was to see how the whole valley had retained much of its beauty.

Emerging from the park I found Tredegar at my feet and walked down to Charles Street where Bevan was born in 1897. The house has gone now, but the home of his sister Arianwen still stands. Here he wrote his great book *In Place of Fear*, published in 1952. His nephew, R. Bevan Norris, has vivid memories of the uncle who was once called by a newspaper 'the Napoleon of Tredegar'.

'I don't know whether all authors are like this,' he smiled, 'but a tremendous amount of whisky was drunk in order to give him inspiration of some sort. I don't think he ate or slept much during that time. He was very tortured by the writing of that book. My mother prepared meals for him, but he never offered to pay and that was always a little niggle.

'I always think of him warmly. I remember he was very relieved that I found *Dr Zhivago* virtually unreadable because he had tried it himself and he did not get on with it either. It was a Technicolor period of our lives when he was around ... and when he died we moved into black and white.'

The Workmen's Medical Aid Society played a large part in the town's story and its imposing Victorian building remains a monument. For a small weekly subscription people could have all the medical treatment they needed, without fear of heavy bills, as well as sickness benefit. It was a pioneer of medical insurance. Alan Fox, who told me about it, said it was equipped with four doctors' surgeries, a nurse, a chiropodist and, in time, a dental surgery and an operating theatre. The doctor-author A.J. Cronin worked for the Society and drew on the experience in his novel *The Citadel*, published in 1937.

'Nye Bevan was hugely influenced by what went on here,' said Alan. 'In Tredegar we like to think that it was a National Health Service in embryo.'

Aneurin Bevan died in 1960. A close friend collected his ashes from the crematorium and drove them to Tredegar. The urn was wrapped in brown paper on the back seat. The friend left the car for a few minutes and while he was away it was stolen. I could imagine his feelings when he returned to find it missing. After a few hours, though, the car was found in a colliery yard and the urn was still on the back seat. Nye's ashes were scattered over his native hills and there is a moving memorial to him above Ebbw Vale.

From almost any place in Tredegar you can see the town clock. Its yellow column on a bright red plinth is like a lighthouse of the valleys. An iron clock for an iron town, it was erected in 1859 in honour of the Iron Duke of Wellington who died in 1852.

You're on Tredegar Time

89

On the way to the town park I passed the house of Michael Foot, who succeeded Bevan as MP for Ebbw Vale. The plaque on the wall notes his long parliamentary service and adds, a proud note I think, 'Biographer of Aneurin Bevan.'

For a while I listened to the town band playing on the bandstand and then went to admire what is claimed to be the largest lump of coal in the world. It weighs 20 tons and was dug by John Jones, nicknamed the Colier Mawr. It was intended for the Great Exhibition of 1851. But when an attempt was made to move it about five tons of it fell off. Instead of going to London it stayed in Tredegar.

I walked south out of town and up the hill to the old cemetery, a Gothic and eerie place where the faded inscriptions on the stumps of gravestones told the story of outbreaks of cholera. I saw that many of those who lie here died young in the 1830s and 1840s. They were hurriedly buried by their fearful families in this bleak hill. Cholera was caused by polluted water but there was a belief at that time that it was spread by a miasma from graves. For that reason chapel and church graveyards were often closed to victims. The cholera cemetery was located on the hill so that the wind would disperse the imagined miasma.

Beyond the gravitational pull of Tredegar, the countryside opened up. Bedwellty Mountain lay ahead, the Rhymney Valley to

The place of fearful burial

the right, the Sirhowy to my left. The wind ruffled the manes of grazing ponies and a lark provided mood music. With a few steps I had reached the wild and lonely paths and left the pavements behind.

The big wheel stopped turning

Descending from the ridge I found a great rusty haulage wheel. It was used to lower quarry stone down the incline. For a hundred years and more the wheel turned and then one day it just stopped and the men left. I wondered if they ever looked back.

The footpath wound down the slope and I crossed the Sirhowy stream. There is nothing to see now of the Bedwellty Pits where, in 1865, 26 men died in an explosion. I climbed up to Troedrhiwgwair and made my way to the Fountain Inn. As I soon discovered, it is more than a pub. It is the heart of the tiny village and a symbol of the community's determination to survive. There is a long story of protest in Troedrhiwgwair. The council felt the village was in danger of being engulfed in a landslide. It was very much a post-Aberfan anxiety. The authorities wanted the people to leave but most of them liked the fellowship of their neighbourly community and loved the view of the valley with the Sirhowy glittering below. Raye Davies, wife of the licensee of the Fountain, told me that the pub opened as a social service – 'it helps to keep us together.'

Troedrhiwgwair flourished in its day. But over the years most of the cottages were pulled down and now there are just the defiant remnants, like little fortresses. One of those who fights on is Brian Gardner. He has put Troedrhiwgwair on the Internet and receives messages from America, Australia and New Zealand, many from people whose parents or grandparents emigrated from the village.

As I left the Fountain one of the customers said: 'They didn't drive us off our lovely mountain. We're still here.'

On the slopes of Cefn Manmoel it was plain to see how the old oak trees had suffered. As oaks they should be sturdy, but the industrial atmosphere made them stunted and puny. But this is a new age. The air is clean, and so are the streams. The colliery scars are fading. In ten years or so it will be as if the mines had never been. There's a sense of justice, of the valleys reclaiming what is rightfully theirs. The modern landscaping marries in with the original agricultural patchwork of hedges and small fields. Lovely country lanes lead over the mountain to Manmoel. As Myra James, who keeps the pub in Manmoel, told me, people looking for respite from the grime and noise have always used these lanes. 'Miners and steelworkers would walk from Ebbw Vale, Tredegar and Markham for the sake of the walk and a drink or two. And when families came on summer weekends it could be like Barry Island here.'

I was on the Sirhowy path now, signposted all the way to Newport, and walking on what was once barren land, a colliery tip. After it was cleared it was soon covered by a junior jungle. Weeds were blossoming in profusion as I walked through: hemlock water dropwort, marsh thistle, lesser stitchwort and Persian speedwell.

On my zigzag way I crossed the Sirhowy again and, emerging from the woods, found the path where the old Sirhowy tram once ran. It was one of the marvels of 1829, the first regular steam engine service in Wales, the locomotive hauling 50 or 60 tons of coal at six miles an hour.

Along its arrow-straight path I walked into the village of Rock. Ewart Smith, a former teacher, told me that in 1834 the local shop was visited by one of the marauding gangs of workers who called themselves the Scotch Cattle. 'They carried lengths of tram rail, stole butter and tobacco and terrified everyone.' The Scotch Cattle roamed in Monmouthshire, Breconshire and Glamorgan and had a bull's head as their emblem. In their unruly way they voiced workers' grievances. 'They were terrorists, yes,' said Ewart, 'but what evolved from the Scotch Cattle was Chartism which led to important reforms of benefit to everyone. It was the first time that a group of men who represented working class discontent had a name.'

One of the pleasures of walking: a well-made bridge

Another bridge, another crossing of the Sirhowy, and I was in Oakdale. It did not grow organically. It was designed as a model town with a pub, church and miners' institute. The old institute was a piece of history, and, taken down stone by stone, has been rebuilt at the Museum of Welsh Life in St Fagans. In the comprehensive school Nigel Jones, the head of music, proudly showed me the platinum disc presented by those old boys of the school, the Manic Street Preachers. They remembered their roots and the school where they had much of their musical education in the choir and the school band.

In Blackwood a plaque marks the place where the Coach and Horses stood. As historian Peter Jones told me, emotions ran high here in November 1839 when a crowd of Chartists gathered to hear the words of their leader John Frost.

'It was miserable and raining as the men crowded together outside the pub. Around seven o'clock a messenger galloped up the street and pushed his way into the bar. A few minutes later John

Frost appeared in a greatcoat, a red scarf around his neck and pistols stuck into his belt. "You all saw that messenger," he said. "He's come from Newport and says the soldiers there are Chartists to a man." There was loud cheering from the crowd and one man called out: "We are enough to eat Newport."

'Frost pushed his way forward and raised his hat, calling "Follow me!" and the disastrous march began.'

Only some of the men knew what was planned, that determined revolution-minded Chartists intended to provoke a full-scale insurrection in a confrontation in Newport. When they learned of the plan, a number of them thought better of it and melted away. In Newport a crowd of around 20,000 massed in front of the Westgate Hotel, facing the troops. Far from being Chartists to a man, the soldiers opened fire and killed 22 of the demonstrators. Frost was among the leaders arrested and transported for life to Australia.

From Blackwood I walked to Gelligroes mill. It is a pretty spot. The miller here in the 1860s, Aneurin Jones, known as Aneurin Fardd (the Poet), went bankrupt and fled to New York to escape his creditors. He started a new life as a gardener and laid out the park at Coney Island. As Principal Supervisor of Parks in Brooklyn, New York, he designed Brooklyn Park arranging, so it is said, for part of it to look just like the view from Gelligroes mill. Aneurin

Gelligroes mill: the news of disaster

Bevan's eisteddfod-minded father was an admirer of his poetry and named his son after him.

The mill is a museum now and in an upstairs room, Howard Moore showed me some early wireless telegraphy equipment. 'My uncle, Artie Moore, was a radio pioneer and very interested in the latest developments, always trying to improve his equipment. This is where he used to work. He was sitting here one night in April 1912 listening to the Morse signals from ships in the North Atlantic when he heard a message from the *Titanic* saying that it had struck an iceberg and was sinking. Through the night the messages became more and more desperate. Next morning my uncle told my grandfather and people in the village. But they did not believe him because they had all read that the *Titanic* was unsinkable. Then the newspapers told the terrible story.'

It was extraordinary that the *Titanic*'s signals had been picked up so far away. No-one realised then that wireless could have such a range. 'My uncle was the only person in Europe to pick up the messages, sitting up here in this mill, unable to do anything.'

Artie Moore's story was reported in the newspapers and he became a local hero. Marconi heard about him and gave him a job, developing and installing marine radios.

On my way up to Mynydd Islwyn I paused at the chapel to see the statue of James Thomas, a Victorian coal owner, posed as if gazing over his kingdom, the stance suggesting a man of importance. From the church at Mynydd Islwyn there is a lovely view of the valley; and, inside, a beautiful window by John Petts augments with grace the church's weather-beaten beauty.

The poet Islwyn (William Thomas) took his name from the mountain. One of those who initiated him into Welsh poetry was Aneurin Fardd. In 1853 Islwyn's fiancée

The artist's purpose

Anne Bowen died and, wrung from his grief, came his most famous poems, both called *Y Storm*.

He married Martha Davies in 1864 but always longed for Anne. It is said that as he died he whispered: 'Thank you, Martha, for all you did for me. You have been very kind. I am going to Anne now.'

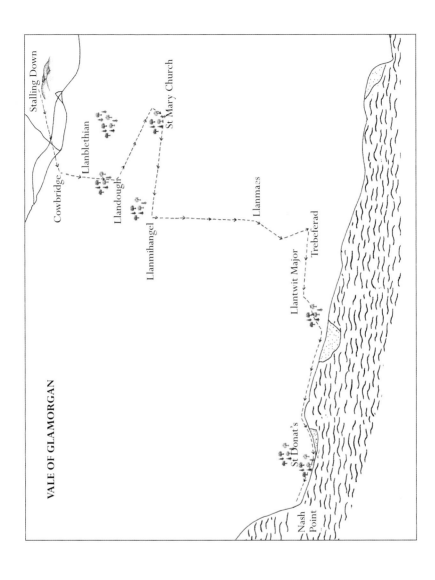

VALE OF GLAMORGAN

Stalling Down

Cowbridge

Llanblethian

Llandough

St Mary Church

Llanmihangel

Llanmaes

Trebeferad

Llantwit Major

St Donat's

Nash Point

9. VALE OF GLAMORGAN

On the mischief trail

The Vale of Glamorgan was braising gently as I set off from Stalling Down, near Cowbridge. Through the skein of crisscross lanes and over downs and meadows I was to zigzag to the sea. The landscape's well-fed look and castle walls stated the principal fact of the Vale, that for centuries it has been desired.

Certainly, no-one adored it more than Edward Williams, better known as Iolo Morganwg, the wayward genius of boundless imagination, who steered between fact and fantasy to bring life to his vision of old Glamorgan.

On Stalling Down in 1795 he called the first Welsh gorsedd, the assembly of the bards of Ancient Britain, the most enduring of his inventions. He had already launched the gorsedd in London. And how did Iolo know the secrets of the bards? Ah, he said, they were whispered to me by a wise man long ago, the last of the old bards. Iolo was nothing if not persuasive.

On the track into Cowbridge I followed in the footsteps of the Romans who marched this way from their base at Caerleon in

Des. res: the luscious Vale

Monmouthshire. Heavily laden with their weapons and accoutrements they had the usual Roman marching target of 10,000 paces a day, the best part of ten miles.

A plaque in the main street of Cowbridge honours Iolo Morganwg, a hero of the town, as 'one of the great benefactors of Welsh letters and history'. More prosaically this was the place where he kept a shop and sold books and groceries. The hieroglyphics at the bottom are drawn from the ancient alphabet of the Welsh bards. We have Iolo's word that there was such an alphabet; but I am afraid that it was one of his fantasies.

Iolo Morganwg, scholar and weaver of words

I crossed the street to the Town Hall, constructed in an age when town halls were magisterial and built to last. It used to be the jail as well and the nine cells are dungeons with thick and heavy doors intended to make a criminal's heart sink. Now it is a museum, the town's fascinating attic, where you can look through the keepsakes and the relics of the centuries. One oddity is a memorial stone erected in gratitude to a horse called Daisy which, at the age of twenty-eight, won a race and died in the moment of victory.

There is also the skeleton of a young man of Roman times. It was discovered when a local car park was excavated; and Marion Eveleigh, the curator, had the job of sorting the boxful of bones. 'All I had to go on,' she said, 'was a photograph of a skeleton.

When I finished a friend of mine, a nurse, came to look and she found only two or three bones in the wrong place.'

On my way out of town, I passed the old Cowbridge Grammar School, founded in the sixteenth century. The poet Alun Lewis, killed in Burma in 1944, was a pupil here; so was the actor Sir Anthony Hopkins. Considered by his schoolfellows to be something of an eccentric, partly for his habit of stretching out on the piano, he was awarded the nickname that endured throughout his schooldays: Mad Hopkins.

A seventeenth-century pupil, Sir Leoline Jenkins, born in Llantrisant, became Principal of Jesus College, Oxford, a famous judge, MP and Secretary of State to Charles II. Samuel Pepys noted his incorruptible character. Sir Leoline also had a fine nose and some say you can tell his descendants by theirs. A portrait of Sir Leoline hangs in the present school and Martin Jenkins, the caretaker, who has been told he has Sir Leoline's noble nose stood beside the picture and allowed me to compare. I fancied there was certainly a similarity. 'There's talk in the family that we are descended from Sir Leoline.' Martin said. 'I think it's a handsome nose ... distinctive.'

At Llanblethian I paused to watch restoration work on the gatehouse which is all that remains of the medieval St Quintin's Castle. Heading out of the orbit of the town, I walked through buttercup meadows to Llandough Castle. Here, said Nigel Anderson, the

The storehouse of meanings

100

owner, the French composer Gabriel Fauré stayed for a while and wrote his haunting Seventh Nocturne.

A handsome house nearby was the home of the Reverend John Walters, curate and later rector of Llandough (who was another Cowbridge Grammar scholar). Tom Warner, who owns the house, told me about Walters's majestic English-Welsh dictionary and showed me the room where he laboured. 'It took him thirty years to complete. He had many difficulties ... he was not wealthy, had to pay the printers and the printers went broke.' The dictionary was printed in 14 parts in Cowbridge and was finally completed and published in London in 1794.

'The work was very hard and he only just survived to see the first edition printed. He had four sons and none of them survived to see the publication.'

Tom showed me the preface to the dictionary and John Walters's poignant memorial to his four boys.

> Adieu, dear Shades! accept, fraternal Band,
> This last, sad tribute from a Father's hand.

He also showed me pages from the diary written by Walters's fourteen-year-old son Daniel in 1775:

> 'At home, busy about my task. Called to see Caleb, who on Tuesday last was hoisted up by the rope of the bell and vastly bruised.'
> 'At school, much discomposed in my spirits, which I impute to the dullness of the weather.'
> 'Went a fishing with Mr William Morgan. Popkin fell into the river and was like to have drowned.'
> 'Went to school, played ball, came home and that's all.'

I crossed the down on the way to the old manor house of Beaupre. Iolo Morganwg loved this place and made up a story about it, claiming that the bards of Glamorgan met here. The artistic heart of the ruin is the Italianate renaissance gateway. As the historian Brian Davies told me, passion lies behind its construction. Two brothers were rivals for the affections of a pretty girl. They quarrelled so violently that she told them she wanted nothing to do with either of them. Disconsolate, one of them went to London, became an apprentice to Italian stonemasons and went with them to Italy. There he learnt the techniques of Italian renaissance archi-

Beaupre: the Italian job

tecture, returned to Wales and offered his services as an architect
and stonemason to the gentry. Maybe it is true; maybe not.

Wherever we walk in the Vale we find ourselves caught up in
Iolo's web of fantasy. You can almost hear his chuckle as we try to
disentangle the wisps of truth that lie somewhere in his fables. At
least in St Mary Church we have some of the true story of Iolo.
He was married here to his devoted Margaret. A couple of years
later he was thrown into Cardiff jail for debt, by no means the first
of his misadventures. His wife knew her husband was a dreamer.
She wrote to him once: 'Dear Ned, you are still building castles in
the air which will crush you under their ruins.'

Iolo was as skilled a carver as he was a poet, scholar and romantic deceiver. A stone in the church, in memory of his father-in-law
Rees Robert ap Rees, testifies to his skill.

The tiny thirteenth-century church at Llanmihangel, lit only by
oil lamps, is a gem. It lies under the protection of a fortified
mansion Plas Llanmihangel, set on a small hill, one of the finest
examples of an early gentry house of Glamorgan. It is mostly
Tudor but parts are seven centuries old. It may well have been
attacked by Owain Glyndwr's forces. David Beer, an architect, and
his wife Sue, saw it by chance during an afternoon drive through

A true craftsman: script by Iolo

Plas Llanmihangel: restored to glory

the Vale in 1987. They fell for it at once and decided to buy and restore it. 'Bed and breakfast guests help to pay for the restoration,' Sue said. 'You don't own a house like this. You can only be the custodian.'

She showed me the portrait upstairs of a solemn girl wearing a blue gown. 'The story is that the portrait is meant to remain here, that anyone who takes it away will have bad luck.'

The path took me south over the fields of Llanmaes to Boverton Place where Iolo Morganwg's mother, Ann Mathews, was raised. She was an orphan at nine, but brought up by a gentry family and given a good education. Clearly she was schooled to be the wife of a country gentleman, but she married a stonemason. Her son was devoted to her.

The small estate of houses at Trebeferad tells part of the story of south Wales in the 1930s. It was built by idealists for unemployed miners, so that men could work above the ground in the sunshine and not beneath it in the dark. One of the first to take up the new life was Howard Smith. 'This all began when the Prince of Wales came to the mining valleys and made his famous '"Something must be done" remark. Miners were picked from the Rhondda and the western valleys to live here and train as market gardeners. The estate was run on socialist principles like a collective farm and managed by a committee chosen by the men. If there was a profit it was paid out as a bonus.'

In the mid-1930s 60 families came to work on the 762-acre communal farm at a rent of four shillings a week.

Llantwit Major's eastern district is modern, but the western part offers a walk through the centuries. The lovely ancient church of St Illtyd gives Llantwit its melodious Welsh name, Llanilltyd Fawr. A curious story lies behind the tall stone at the back of the church. Few people believed Iolo Morganwg when he said that the stone, known as the Pillar of Samson, had marked the grave of a giant, a village youth seven feet and seven inches tall, and that the stone had in time fallen into the grave. Iolo started digging near the church and found the stone. It has distinctive Celtic carving and bears the name of Illtyd. From this Iolo wove a tale of a paradise in the Vale of Glamorgan, filled with princes, poets, saints, colleges and beauty. Many of the Vale's inhabitants will say modestly that nothing has changed.

I walked to the coast where the Vale merges with the sea among great rock barriers and spectacular cliffs and deep caves. Inside one

Where to find a wife in Glamorgan

of the caves I hurled some pebbles over the Arch of Destiny, in salute to the story that a man who throws six stones over the arch will marry the girl he is with.

St Donat's Castle has a grand pedigree. It was the seat of the Stradlings, conquerors of Glamorgan, was started in the fourteenth century and has always been occupied. In 1962 it became Atlantic College, the first of a number of pioneering international schools.

It was restored in the 1930s by William Randolph Hearst, the American newspaper tycoon, who spent a million pounds improving the plumbing, a very American thing to do. For a while he imported Hollywood to Wales, and stars like Charlie Chaplin came to St Donat's to lark at his expense.

In St Donat's church, Alan Hall, a teacher at Atlantic College, told me about Sir Thomas Stradling. 'He was the last of the Stradlings and is buried here with his father and brother. He was killed in a duel in Montpelier in 1738. He had gone on a Grand Tour with Sir John Tyrwhitt as his companion and each man signed a will leaving his property to the other, to my mind an invitation to be killed.

'The body was brought back to St Donat's, which must have taken a long time in those days and two stories are told about it. The first was that the body lay in state in the Great Hall and

St Donat's: devoted Stradlings

candles set fire to the hangings, causing a blaze which destroyed many Stradling family portraits. The second is that Sir Thomas's old nurse lifted the coffin lid and saw that the fingers of the corpse were all intact. But she knew that when he was a boy Sir Thomas had a finger bitten off by a donkey.

'Many retainers at the castle refused to believe that Sir Thomas had been killed and that the family line was at an end. But both of these stories were told by Taliesin, son of Iolo, who readily mixed fact and fiction,' Alan said.

In the churchyard I saw the grave of Mary Morgan. She was a tenant of the lord of the manor and when they quarrelled he evicted her. 'But I shall be buried here,' she promised him. A few years later he died and was buried in the churchyard. But later his remains were disinterred and reburied near Neath. And while the grave at St Donat's was open Mary Morgan died and was buried in it. She won in the end.

I walked in bright sunshine to the gleaming white lighthouse at Nash Point, a familiar and welcome landmark for countless navigators in the hazardous Bristol Channel. It was erected after a ship struck rocks and sank with great loss of life in 1830.

A nineteenth-century antiquarian told the story of a wine ship

Nash Point: son et lumière

running aground here, strewing barrels of wine along the shore. He said he found a woman lying on her back on the beach, as merry as a lark, and each time a wave splashed over her face she said: 'Oh, no more thank you. I've had quite enough.'

Along this stretch of coast there is the second greatest tidal range in the world. I watched the retreating waters of the Bristol Channel unveil the extraordinary rock pavements beneath the layered bulwarks of the cliffs, one of the wonders of Wales.

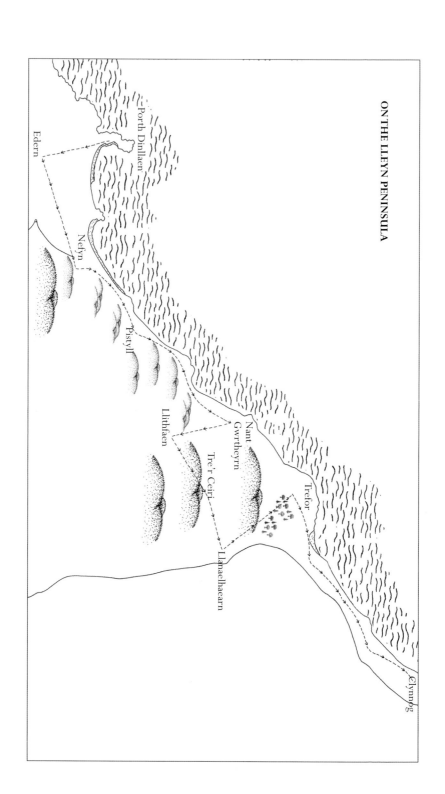

ON THE LLEYN PENINSULA

Porth Dinllaen

Edern

Nefyn

Pistyll

Llithfaen

Nant
Gwrtheyrn

Tre'r Ceiri

Trefor

Llanaelhaearn

Clynnog

10. ON THE LLEYN PENINSULA

From here to Cape Horn

From the hill on the promontory I looked down on the slated roofs of Porth Dinllaen, sheltered in the scimitar curve of its sandy bay. The visionary William Madocks had big ambitions for this modest place and it stands today as one of the might-have-beens of history. Madocks intended it to be the harbour serving the ships on the London to Dublin stage coach and ferry route he planned. But Parliament chose Holyhead instead and the story goes that Porth Dinllaen lost out by only one parliamentary vote.

The weather was bright and very blustery as I walked along the edge of the golf course. In 1881 the steamer *Cyprian* was wrecked on the rocks here. As the ship was breaking up Captain John Strachan found a stowaway on board, a young boy. The captain took off his lifebelt and strapped it onto him. The boy was saved. The captain drowned. A tribute to his nobility was paid in Westminster Abbey.

Some of the crew of the *Cyprian* were buried in Edern churchyard. The church itself is small and simple. A plaque near the altar tells us something about country life years ago. The men of the

Porth Dinllaen: not enough votes

Griffith family of Cefnamlwch died young and left no sons, so the property went to the daughters. It happened in many landed families. A writer in 1810 provided a simple explanation: 'The women were sober ... the men drank themselves to death. For this habit some apology may be found in the remoteness of the situation and the rusticity of manners.'

Along the road I met Peter Heywood, a beekeeper. He invited me to see his beehives in a nearby glade. He fitted me up with a veiled hat, like his own, so that we looked like a couple of dames off to Ascot races. Peter keeps his bees in the old fashioned way, in straw houses called skeps, and to my eye they resembled miniatures of straw houses in parts of Africa. Peter lifted one of the skeps to show me the teeming bees inside and the honeycombs they had made.

'Fifty thousand bees in each hive,' he said. He carried a smoke-maker with him and allowed smoke to drift over the bees. 'In their natural state they live in hollow trees and the smoke to them seems like a forest fire. Their reaction is to consume as much honey as they can, ready to flee. But when they are full of honey, as they are now, they find it difficult to sting you. So they don't.'

In the distance rose the blue trident peaks of Yr Eifl, their name long ago anglicised into The Rivals.

All abuzz: housing in the bee-loud glade

A walk through a long green valley brought me to Nefyn. Edward I was fond of this village and in 1284 chose it for his cele-bration of victory over the princes of north Wales. There was a tournament with jousting knights, feasting and music. The dancing was so exuberant that the floor collapsed, sending the dancers tumbling to the floor below. The occasion is still recalled in the name of a meadow, Cae Ymryson, Tournament Field.

Clement Attlee, Prime Minister after the Second World War, often enjoyed a holiday at a house in Nefyn owned by his wife's family. His photograph is in many a local album and I was shown a picture of him standing in his baggy and very British seaside shorts. Naturally, the pictures show that summers were much sunnier in those days.

Even in a holiday retreat, the business of state had to go on. Telephones in the 1940s were rather primitive and it was not always easy to make a long-distance call through the operator. One day, Attlee's secretary said to the village switchboard operator: 'I'm speaking for the Prime Minister. He must have a line to London.' And the operator responded: 'And I'm speaking for the Postmas-ter General, bach. The Prime Minister will have to wait his turn.'

I climbed to the top of the lookout tower from which a watch

The sailors' pin-up: Nefyn museum

Art of the Roaring Forties: a ship on a feather

was kept for ships and fishing boats. Nefyn once owed much of its living to the herring shoals which frequented this coast. Indeed, herrings were known as Nefyn beef and were said to have 'bellies like innkeepers and backs like farmers'. That is why the village has a herring on its coat of arms and a herring for a wind vane. But the herring, here as elsewhere, were overfished and by 1914 had ceased to come into the bay.

Nefyn was for centuries a kingdom of ships and seafarers and its story is well told in the museum set up in the old church. This is the village's memory. As well as breeding sailors, Nefyn built fine ships on the beach, nearly 200 of them in the years from 1810 to 1880. One builder employed 300 carpenters.

The museum houses models and pictures of the ships and figureheads, flags, paintings and ships' gear. There is also a unique photographic gallery of Nefyn men, scores of them, a whole tribe of master mariners who learnt their latitude and longitude as they learnt their ABC before following their fathers and brothers to the sea. This remarkable collection shows us square, capable men, feet planted sturdily on the quarterdeck: Joneses, Jenkinses, Hugheses, Evanses and Llewellyns – what a contribution they made to British seafaring.

Captain Evan Morris had more than his share of adventure. Washed overboard in a storm off Newfoundland, he swam back on board and had his leg broken by the ship's wheel which was spinning freely. But he grasped the wheel and brought the vessel under control. Another of his ships caught fire near Cape Horn and he was 19 days in an open boat before reaching the Falklands. He ended a mutiny aboard another ship by shooting the ringleader.

Such men saw the world when seafaring was frequently a dangerous adventure and distant places were truly exotic. Many people in Nefyn treasure the curios seamen brought home and the pictures of ships they served in.

Mary O'Shea showed me a picture of a ship under full sail. 'This is one of the vessels my grandfather captained,' she said. 'He had a son born on board, 19 days out of Southampton, and named him Seaborn. And here is my grandfather's last ship on which he had another son and called him Ocean.'

From a chest she brought the yellow foot of an albatross and a long, shining black pigtail. Her uncle dived overboard to save a drowning Chinese seaman and the man cut off his pigtail, his great pride, and gave it to his rescuer as a symbol of his gratitude. Mrs O'Shea's neighbour Gwenda Williams showed me the simple arts, painting and carving, with which sailors passed away the hours.

Bidding farewell to Cape Horn I resumed my journey along the paths of Lleyn. Soon I was at Pistyll, the favourite holiday place of the actor Rupert Davies who lies buried in the churchyard, forever Maigret, the pipe-smoking French detective he brought brilliantly to life in many television episodes.

I walked down to Nant Gwrtheyrn. This part of Lleyn is granite country, the best and most durable granite in Britain. Just as

Along the granite coast

Welsh slate put a roof over heads, so Welsh granite put a road beneath the feet. It paved the streets of Victorian London, Liverpool, Manchester and many other cities. Quarrying started at Nant in the 1850s and the first workers were housed in barracks. As the business prospered cottages were built and workers brought their wives to live with them, swelling the population to 200. A chapel and a school completed the picture. The steep and winding track into the village made bulk deliveries difficult, though the men found ways of getting barrels of beer for the weekend, and coal and food were often delivered by the ships which called to load the granite. People sometimes went by sea to Liverpool to do their shopping.

When the quarrying finished, in the 1930s, Nant fell silent. But it began a new life in the 1970s. Under the leadership of Dr Carl Clowes, a local GP determined to strengthen the Welsh-speaking community, the Nant Gwrtheyrn Trust bought the village and established it as a centre for teaching Welsh. Thousands have been here to take the linguistic plunge and the once empty village is lively with talk.

Thirsty quarrymen used to leave publess Nant and toil up the path to Llithfaen to drink at the Victoria, better known as Tafarn y Fic. It now belongs to the local people who bought it, just as they did the village shop, to support life in the village. When I called for a drink I found some of the customers painting the doors and windows: if you drink the beer, you are expected to slap on a little paint, too, in the spirit of community.

'We wanted to do something ourselves to keep a Welsh way of life full of vigour,' said Gwenan Williams. 'Local people got the money together to buy the Vic ... and that's when the hard work started.'

Ioan Mai Evans, who lives in Llithfaen, showed me a derelict cottage on the edge of the village. It was the home of a forgotten hero. In 1812 Robert William Hughes led a protest to stop the local squires enclosing the common land, calling villagers out with a conch shell to pelt surveyors and drive them off. Soldiers were sent to restore order.

'Robert Hughes was arrested, tried at Caernarfon, sentenced to death and eventually transported to Australia. He died there aged seventy,' said Ioan. 'To my mind he was a hero and deserves to be remembered.'

From the cottage I walked the long track to the eastern peak of Yr Eifl hillside to explore Tre'r Ceiri, the Town of Giants. This is the best preserved Iron Age town in England and Wales and it is not too difficult to get your imagination to people it. The gateway and huts

Tre'r Ceiri: Iron Age avenue

and the walls recently restored by Cadw provide a real sense of those who dwelt here in the second century while the Romans marched far below. It is a truly wild place with tremendous views of Snowdonia and Cardigan Bay.

In Llanaelhaearn Mrs Glennys Hughes showed me a self-portrait of her great-grandfather Robert Hughes. A man of humble beginnings, he became a Methodist minister and, self taught, an artist with his own distinctive style who painted more than 100 portraits in the 1870s and 1880s. The art historian Peter Lord told me about him. 'He did not start painting until he was fifty and made his first portrait by dipping his finger in lamp black and delineating the face of a chapel minister. Everyone recognised it. The glory of his work is his innocent eye, the ability to see his neighbours with a clarity and insight that the touring painters who looked at Wild Wales could not achieve.'

I followed the granite trail to the town of Trefor, named after the first manager of the local quarry, Mr Trefor Jones. Only seven years after the village was founded, in 1856, the brass band was started. It has always been its pride and heartbeat. One of the leading bands of Wales, it has helped to give a big name to a small place. I listened to the Trefor sound as Geraint Jones, the band master, conducted rehearsals.

During a break he told me of the competition incident of 1895. 'The Gwynedd eisteddfod was held in Pwllheli that year and the bands were competing in a quick step marching contest. They had to march down the High Street from the Crown to the Whitehall Hotel where the adjudicator sat at an open window. The bands were meant to march off at four minute intervals, but unfortunately the second band was despatched too soon and marched straight into the unfinished performance of the first band. And then the Trefor band was sent off, also too early, and went into the other bands. Fiasco. A battle on the street.'

With tempers frayed and the bands and their angry supporters brawling, a magistrate was summoned to read the Riot Act to restore peace.

Clynnog church: pilgrims and barking dogs

Along the beach, I was guided in by the reassuring square tower of Clynnog church. Christianity made an early mark at this place. A church was built in the seventh century, a refreshment stop for pilgrims on their way to Bardsey, the little drop at the end of Lleyn's nose. For those early pilgrims three trips to Bardsey were worth one to Rome.

ON THE LLEYN PENINSULA

In the church I read something of the story of Edgar Christian, who left the village in 1926, at the age of seventeen. He went to join his mother's cousin Jack Hornby and another man, Harold Adlard, on a expedition to the aptly-named Barren Lands in northern Canada.

Wilfred Williams, who has made a study of the story, told me that Jack Hornby was an experienced hunter and gold prospector and expected to find plenty of caribou to hunt, ensuring a stock of meat to last through the winter.

'But when they reached the Thelon River they found they were too late. The caribou had gone.'

Far from help, Edgar and his companions sheltered in an old log cabin, hoping to survive by trapping and hunting. The temperature fell to minus 50C. The men found nothing to eat. Gradually they starved. Jack Hornby died exhausted, then Harold Adlard. Edgar survived for another month and somehow kept a diary. It was found by a search party of the Royal Canadian Mounted Police.

The last entry, in June 1927, said: 'Sunshine is bright now. See if that does any good to me if I get out and bring in wood to make fire tonight. Got out. Too weak and all in now. Left things late.'

Edgar's father published the diary under the title *Unflinching*. It became a classic, once known to every Canadian child, a story of courage in the shadow of death.

On the wall of the church hung a set of dog tongs. Years ago shepherds and farmers were inseparable from their dogs. They worked together. They went to church together. But the hymns and sermons were sometimes drowned by the barking of dogs; and, it has to be said, mischievous boys sometimes goaded the dogs to bark when the sermon was dull. That was when the churchwarden reached for his trusty tongs, grasped the delinquent dogs by their necks and threw them out. The tongs were meant to handle the most Baskervillean of hounds. Their bite was definitely worse than the bark.

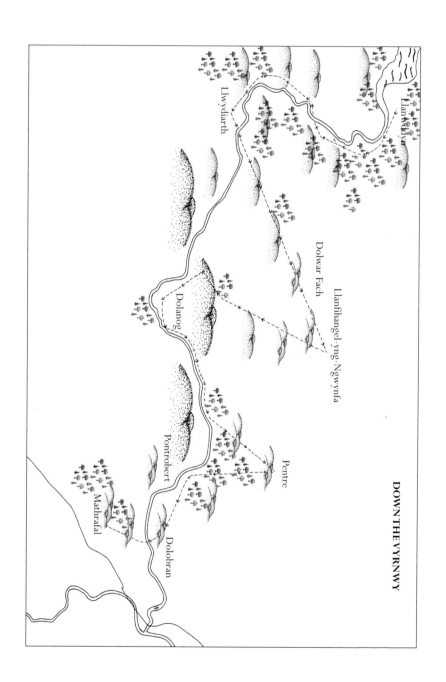

DOWN THE VYRNWY

Llanwddyn

Llwydiarth

Dolwar Fach

Llanfihangel-yng-Ngwynfa

Dolanog

Pontrobert

Pentre

Mathrafal

Dolobran

11. DOWN THE VYRNWY

Words remembered

In the 1860s the rapidly growing city of Liverpool cast around anxiously for a new source of water. Several lakes and rivers were considered but the favoured scheme was the damming of the River Vyrnwy. When Parliament approved it in 1880 an army of 1,000 men advanced on the valley. Using the latest technology of steam cranes to haul up massive stones, they built the first major masonry dam in Britain. It held back the largest artificial reservoir in Europe.

Wall of water

The waters drowned the village of Llanwddyn, with its three pubs, two chapels, one church, ten farms and a post office, a community of more than 400 people. The villagers saved what they could, stripped the slates from the chapel, posed for a farewell photograph and moved into new homes downstream.

They also took with them the bones of their ancestors. Four hundred graves were opened and the bones reburied in the grounds of the rather stolid new church built by Liverpool Corporation in 1888 to replace the old one. The people also carted with

The architect's fancy: the control tower on Vyrnwy

Water for the city

them a souvenir of the village sports, a stone weighing 75½ pounds, and it now rests on a window ledge of the church. A mighty man called Llewellyn Fawr once hurled it 45 feet, a throw never bettered.

Vyrnwy's water first flowed to Liverpool in 1892 and the four-mile lake soon grew as a tourist attraction. When I started my walk at the dam the water shone with a hard diamond brightness. At other times, walled by gloomy pines, it has a certain brooding grandeur. A century ago the dam was admired as a triumph of Victorian engineering; though later, to many minds, the drowning of valleys represented profound loss.

Soon I was in rugged countryside, among the characteristic steep hills and swift streams of this landscape. I found no bridge to take me easily over the River Vyrnwy and I took off my boots to wade through clear and icy water on stones as slippery as soap. The beauty of these uplands can be deceptive. Lovely in summer, they can be cruelly harsh in winter. A chilling wind that swirls from the Berwyn hills was called by some frozen poet 'the wind of dead men's feet'. The name itself is enough to make you shiver.

I crossed the fields to Llwydiarth, a mansion that once marked the status and style of a branch of the Vaughan family, famous patrons of poets in the sixteenth century. On a low hill at the back of the house I found Professor Barri Jones at work. An archaeologist at Manchester University, he was investigating a maze whose outlines he had first discovered in an aerial survey.

From ancient times mazes have symbolised magic and spiritual experience and often represented a pilgrimage or a journey through life. Certainly, mazes were built in ancient Celtic times, but the labyrinth at Llwydiarth was probably part of an ornamental garden laid out when the Vaughans flourished. Its walls were of turf and it is one of about a dozen such mazes known in Britain.

Although Professor Jones used electronic sounders to trace the outline of the maze, he had the assistance of Val Worden, a dowser. With a copper rod in each hand, her eyes closed in concentration, she walked slowly over the site. The rods swung gently to indicate the lines of the maze.

'They are reacting to the earth banks of the maze,' he said. 'They can trace the outline just as efficiently as our modern detectors. We have been getting remarkable results.'

Farmer John Owen lives in the big house at Llwydiarth, once the home of squires. The old order is turned upside down. 'I'm the descendant of tenant farmers,' mused John, 'and my grandfather would be amazed to see his family living here. He wouldn't have dreamed it could happen.'

In the village of Llanfihangel-yng-Ngwynfa – the Church of

Ann Griffiths: the singing heart

Michael in Paradise – an obelisk marks the grave of the remarkable Ann Griffiths. A farmer's daughter and farmer's wife, she was a woman blessed. Young, exuberant and a lover of dancing, she was also a mystic, a great hymn writer and poet. Her work survives by a remarkable chance.

Ann was born in 1776 and died in 1805 aged twenty-nine. She lived at Dolwar Fach farm, in the confines of an isolated Montgomeryshire valley, two miles from Llanfihangel. We know that she travelled to Llanfyllin, six miles off, and to Bala, 22 miles away, but not much farther. She never even saw the sea. Her spirit, however, sang to a wider world.

Canon Donald Allchin came to Llanfihangel to talk to me about Ann. A noted religious scholar, he knew nothing of her until he came to Wales on holiday years ago and heard her story. He was enchanted by it and his studies led him to write movingly of her life.

He believes that she has a unique place in the spiritual history of Britain. 'There is nobody like her as a woman hymn writer,' he told me. 'No-one can begin to hold a candle to her.' Ann had a philosophical turn of mind, he said, and pondered the great questions of human existence, fulfilment and destiny. 'It is extraordinary ... she lived in a little farm house in a remote valley, yet in her heart and mind she was travelling far beyond the stars and this world.'

Llanfihangel: postman's nook

In many ways Llanfihangel is a charming retreat, a private place. The post box is secreted in the porch of a house. And as for The Goat, the modest village pub, it is hardly like a pub at all. Walk in for a glass of beer and you find yourself in the cosiness of the landlady's sitting room, a guest among the family mementoes, the photographs on the piano. It is very much an amiable and informal community pub and Menna Rowlands, whose family has been running it for four generations, told me it would not change. 'We like it as it is, comfortable and a bit old-fashioned; and our customers feel the same.'

I called at the studio of Keith Breeden. He used to be a designer of record covers but now he is doing what he really wants, earning his living as an artist. He is a vigorous supporter of the way of life in the village. His first major work was a portrait of two local farmers, bachelor brothers Jack and Morley Richards. It won a prize at the National Portrait Gallery. Keith painted the brothers on their hillside smallholding, the ten acres where they have lived all their lives, as much a part of the rugged land as the trees. The portraits are of individuals but they represent a breed of hardy men.

The hedgerows were at their floral best as I walked the lanes. There were dog roses, black bryony, pink petals of sweet briar, yellow meadow vetch and tufted vetch, too: a whole florist's shop

... and the fragrance of honeysuckle.

I followed what used to be a drovers' track along which Welsh cowboys drove their sheep and cattle from the hills to the markets of Wales and England. It unrolled like a green carpet towards Dolwar Fach, the home of Ann Griffiths, a working farm today just as it was when she became mistress of it on her mother's death. When she was twenty-one Ann became a passionate convert to Methodism and her home became a centre of Methodist teaching. The descendants of the family which moved into the farm a year after Ann died are still there and see themselves as stewards of history. For two centuries they have welcomed pilgrims.

Linda Jones, who took me around the house, showed me the visitors' books which date back to 1909. 'People come from all over

Songs of praise

the world. We always take them around.' The books form a monument to the way Ann Griffiths has touched many hearts.

In the chapel in Dolanog I saw the memorial to Ann; and the bas-relief of her face, the only known likeness. She died less than a year after her marriage to Thomas Griffiths, only two weeks after the birth and death of her daughter.

Walking east along the glorious valley, I could see the land where, in 1818, a quarrel erupted between two men cutting corn. A sickle flashed and one of them fell, his backbone cut through. The killer was Edward Thomas, brother of Ann Griffiths. He was jailed for a year for manslaughter. After his release he became a Sunday school teacher near Merthyr Tydfil and rebuilt his good name; another of the family marked by passion and faith.

Branching up to Pentre I came to a seventeenth-century house being restored by Ron and Christine Gilson. They pointed out some curious small circular marks carved on the beams. 'They were put there to keep witches out,' Ron explained. 'There used to be a strong fear of witches coming down the chimney or through the doors. They work – we've never had a witch in here.'

Christian conviction has led a number of people from this district to distant parts of the world. Thomas Jones went to the remote Khasi hills of North East India in 1841 to work as a missionary and is revered to this day as the father of Khasi literature and founder of the Khasi Methodist church. The people there still sing to Welsh hymn tunes. The renowned John Davies, who came from Pendugwm farm, was a friend

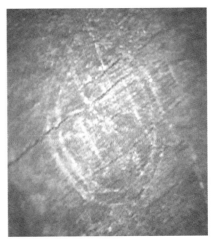

On your broomstick

of Ann Griffiths and influenced her thinking. When he was twenty-nine he became a missionary in Tahiti and worked there until he died fifty-four years later. He translated parts of the bible into Tahitian and was always known as John Davies Tahiti.

Pontrobert is a crucial link with the story of Ann Griffiths. Only a few of her hymns were ever written down and only one hymn and one letter written in her hand have survived. However, Ruth Hughes, her maid and companion at Dolwar Fach, knew all the hymns by heart. She was illiterate. After Ann's death Ruth dictated them to her husband, the Reverend John Hughes, and they were published in 1806.

John Hughes and Ruth lived next door to the chapel in Pontrobert. The centrepiece of the building is the pulpit where John Hughes preached so powerfully. In the 1980s the chapel was a ruin but it was restored as an interdenominational centre. It is fitting that the John Hughes chapel should have this role, for he was a spiritual force in the valley and a mentor to Ann Griffiths and others.

Nia Rhosier, a moving spirit in the restoration of the chapel, showed me a little brown door, about the size of a serving hatch, high up in the chapel wall. 'When John Hughes was ill and unable to come down into the chapel to preach, that door was opened so that he could do so from his bed.' In this fashion, eking out his energy, he preached until the end.

Walking south west, I saw a good stand of oak trees in the

Top left, the preacher's sermon hatch

Dolobran: Quakers' refuge

distance. Some of the timber was used in the new Globe Theatre by the Thames. Nearby is Dolobran, home of the Lloyd family. Sampson Lloyd founded Lloyd's bank in 1765. In the seventeenth century the Lloyds were persecuted for their Quaker beliefs: it was a time when Quakers were jailed and their property confiscated. But in 1700, in a quiet almost secret hollow, they built a little meeting house which is still used and still carefully maintained. It is eloquent in its simplicity.

A member of the family, Father Charles Lloyd, still lives in Dolobran, guarding the history and keeping track of the scattered tribe of Lloyds.

'We have been on this site since 1405, except for a hundred years when the estate was bankrupt and it had to be bought back. And we were living farther up the valley from 1320. I recently met an offshoot from the family which split in 1405 and worked out that we were 24th cousins.'

I finished on the tree-crowned tump at Mathrafal, where the rivers Vyrnwy and Banwy meet. This was the chief court of the princes of Powys. I had to imagine their pomp. Here they feasted, swaggered and listened to their bards who, ransacking their stores of rhymes, no doubt praised the beauty of the valley and the grace, wisdom and nobility of its rulers.

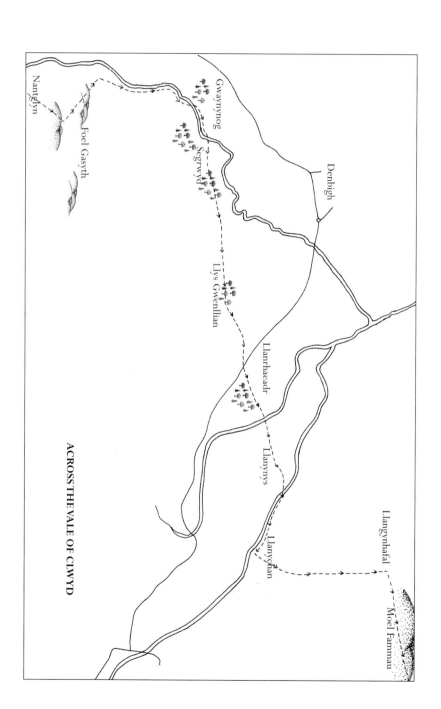

ACROSS THE VALE OF CLWYD

Nantglyn

Foel Gasyth

Gwaynynog

Segrwyd

Denbigh

Llys Gwenllian

Llanrhaeadr

Llanynys

Llanychan

Llangynhafal

Moel Fammau

12. ACROSS THE VALE OF CLWYD

Oh, Cecilia

Nantglyn was my starting point, a link with the Pacific Ocean and Captain Cook, the greatest of navigators.

David Samwell was born here in 1751, the son of a parson. He trained as a naval surgeon and sailed in the *Resolution* on the third and last of James Cook's epic voyages. He was a good shipmate, sunny, amusing and, as many parsons' sons are, irreverent. He kept a lively journal which detailed the enjoyments as well as the hardships of ocean exploration. He had a roving eye, too, and deeply admired 'the Dear Girls' encountered in the islands. At the same time he was very serious about his profession and his literary interests. He was close by when Cook was hacked to death in Hawaii in 1779 and wrote a book about the voyage and its tragic end. He was a poet, with the bardic name of Dafydd Ddu Feddyg, Black David the Doctor, and a pillar of the London Welsh. He knew Iolo Morganwg and, with him, was a founder of the Gorsedd, or the Bards of Britain, which first met on Primrose Hill, in London, in 1792.

Across the Vale to Denbigh

Rather than walk the road towards Denbigh, I climbed Foel Gasyth and was rewarded by a panorama of hills. Denbigh Castle rose about four miles distant, sternly commanding the landscape. Elian Jones joined me here to put me on the right path. She knows the area better than most, for she was the last postman to deliver the mail on foot to the outlying farms, walking 15 miles a day, six days a week, in all weathers.

'Dogs were always a problem and I still have the tooth marks on my hands. There was a particular dog who would always bite if I faced him, so one day I decided to walk backwards to the farmhouse door. That worked all right until I bent down to put the letters through the box. Then he bit me on my bottom.'

To those on remote farms Elian was a welcome sight, a trusted confidante, a reliable and resourceful friend. 'Quite a few people were not good at reading and writing and dealing with official business. I used to help them fill in forms and sort out business matters. They asked me to read their letters to them and write the replies and even the cheques.'

Segrwyd Mill, near the Ystrad River bridge, closed more than forty years ago, the last flour mill in the valley. When I stepped inside it was as if the work stopped only yesterday. John Lloyd, the former miller, met me there to talk about the old days. He was in his nineties and his memory had a long reach. He explained that country mills like his were built to handle modest cart loads of grain, not bulk lorry loads. It was modernisation, the growth in transport capacity, that stopped the water wheel and ended the miller's way of life.

'We were paid in corn, not cash,' he said, 'about ten pounds weight for every hundred we ground. We fed it to the pigs and hens which we sold to raise money.'

He returned often to look at the mill and its machinery, he said. 'And the funny thing is that when I dream, my dreams are always of the mill.'

Walking the meadows beside the Ystrad stream I found Dr Johnson's Monument in the shelter of some trees. It was a rather odd construction to see in this out of the way place, an urn set on a pedestal and inscribed with these flowery words:

'This spot was often dignified by the presence of Samuel Johnson whose moral writings, exactly conformable to the precepts of Christianity give ardour to virtue and confidence to truth.'

It was erected by Colonel John Myddleton of nearby

Dear Doctor... words in the meadow

Gwaynynog to commemorate Dr Johnson's visit in 1774. The great lexicographer, however, disapproved of the monument and grumbled that it looked like an attempt to bury him alive.

Dr Johnson was touring Wales with his friend Mrs Hester Thrale when he arrived to stay at Gwaynynog. The personable Mrs Thrale was a friend of writers and artists, and for sixteen years Dr Johnson lodged with her and Mr Thrale in their home in London.

After dining with Colonel Myddleton Dr Johnson noted in his diary that 'the table was well supplied, except the fruit was bad. It was truly the dinner of a country gentleman'.

Janie Smith, who owns the house, told me that on another occasion Dr Johnson interfered with the dinner arrangements. 'Colonel Myddleton summoned the gardener to bring in a live hare which was to be cooked for dinner. Dr Johnson was intrigued. He took it in his arms and stroked it and talked about the wonders of wild life. Bit by bit, he edged towards the open window. He kept Colonel Myddleton talking and, just as the colonel said the hare should be taken back to the kitchen to be cooked, Dr Johnson pushed it through the window. Deprived of his dinner delicacy, Colonel Myddleton was furious.'

Janie's daughter, Frances Williams, showed me the kitchen garden, a re-creation of the Victorian garden Beatrix Potter knew.

The world of Peter Rabbit

Beatrix spent holidays here with her uncle and aunt from 1895 to1913. She made many sketches and paintings of the countryside and the house and garden for the Peter Rabbit books that captured the hearts of generations of children. The top window of the potting shed, for example, is just like that of Mr McGregor's shed in *The Tale of the Flopsy Bunnies*.

I asked Frances if there were still numerous rabbits on the land. 'Yes,' she said, 'but we don't make rabbit pie.'

They couldn't, really, could they?

A path beside a cornfield descended gently towards Denbigh, but I skirted the town and headed into the Vale of Clwyd, aiming for the hills on the far side. I passed a pretty Elizabethan house in which a Mr and Mrs Myddleton raised a crop of nine sons, all of whom prospered in business. The most successful of them was Thomas. He made fortunes in the East India Company and the new American colonies, bought Chirk Castle in 1595 and became Lord Mayor of London in 1613.

Now I found myself bumping into Dr Johnson's travelling companion, Mrs Thrale. She was widowed in 1781 and three years later, to Dr Johnson's distress, married an Italian musician, Gabriel Piozzi. Mrs Piozzi, as she now was, decided to move to Wales with

Segrwyd: a scandalous mistress

her daughter Cecilia. They stayed at the Crown in Denbigh while their house was painted and renovated. In the Crown, Cecilia met John Mostyn and he fell for her. No wonder: Cecilia was a girl and a half, eighteen years old, attractive, adventurous and used to getting her own way. She was also an heiress. John Mostyn courted her for all he was worth. The suspicious Mrs Piozzi wrote in her diary that he 'flirts with Cecilia in hope of securing £50,000 besides a pedigree'.

The house called Segrwyd is part of the Cecilia saga and David Hooson who lives there now told me what happened next.

'Mrs Piozzi thought Mostyn totally inappropriate as a son-in-law and decided to take Cecilia back to London and plunge her into London society so that she could forget this hayseed who was lusting after her. She and Cecilia set off for London but Mostyn trailed them. When they made an overnight stop at Shrewsbury, Mostyn, in the best tradition, climbed up to Cecilia's room on a ladder, extricated her from her bedroom and ran away with her to Gretna Green. There, presumably, they married. Eventually Cecilia, Mostyn and Mrs Piozzi had to go back to Denbigh and make the best of things. Mostyn and Cecilia began to restore Segrwyd with Mrs Piozzi's money.'

It became clear after a while that the couple had unusual domestic arrangements. 'Cecilia was quite happy to share her husband with her maid and Mrs Piozzi was incensed to find that both her daughter and the maid were pregnant at the same time. She insisted that Mostyn set up the maid in a house in Denbigh.'

For all the early passion, Cecilia and Mostyn did not make a happy marriage. The despairing Mrs Piozzi called it all 'a wasps' nest'. After ten years and two separations Mostyn died in Bath. Cecilia lived on at Segrwyd and brought up her children. Mr Hooson showed me the beautiful walled garden she built. Mrs Piozzi, meanwhile, found contentment with her musician on the other side of the valley.

Down the road I came to Llys Gwenllian, a name that goes back seven centuries. There really was a llys, or court, here. Behind the farmhouse is the mound on which there stood a fort that belonged to Gwenllian, the daughter of Llywelyn the Last. A quarrel over this land was part of the resentment that Llywelyn's unpredictable brother Dafydd harboured against Edward I of England. He thought he should have been better rewarded for siding with the king. Out of Dafydd's dissatisfaction grew the struggle in which Llywelyn was killed in 1282. Dafydd, for a few months the last Prince of Wales, was executed in 1283; and Wales fell to Edward.

This may hurt a little

A path across the fields brought me to the home of Dr Gwyn Thomas, a country GP whose father and grandfather practised in Denbigh. He has kept their instruments, and many others, a collection that is part of the history of medicine. 'Every doctor had a set like this,' he said, picking up a polished wooden case of saws, knives, scalpels and clamps. 'And when necessary he would perform operations with them on a farmhouse kitchen table.'

He showed me the chloroform and ether mask, rather like a tea strainer, that doctors put over their patients' noses to anaesthetise them. 'I have seen my father give anaesthetic like this. He would be at the head of the operating table in the Denbighshire Infirmary, giving anaesthetic and reciting Welsh poetry, while the surgeon did a Caesarean, singing Welsh hymns. They made a good combination.'

Dr Thomas demonstrated the working of an ingenious instrument for capturing and cutting off tonsils; and a probe for retrieving a coin stuck in a child's gullet. 'If you could not pull the coin up you pushed it down into the stomach ... and a couple of days later you got the change.'

The poet John Betjeman used to say that the test of a church was: 'Is it worth cycling 12 miles against the wind to see it?' In the case of Llanrhaeadr church the answer is emphatically 'Yes.' A fine

Llanrhaeadr: the window saved from the Roundheads

135

porch and carved roof form part of its beauty, but the chief treasure is its Jesse window, a masterpiece of sixteenth-century stained glass, perhaps the finest in Britain. It shows the line of David growing from the breast of his father Jesse. Its survival is fortunate. To save it from being smashed by Roundhead soldiers in the Civil War the local people dismantled it and hid it in a chest, still to be seen in the church, and buried it in a wood. It was just as well. The east window of the church was not hidden and was destroyed by Cromwellian troops.

Among the memorials in the church a window in the south wall honours James Vaughan Horne, a respectable Denbigh solicitor who died in 1848. A persistent story says that he was the father of Sir Henry Morton Stanley, the journalist and explorer of Africa who famously found Dr Livingstone in 1876. Stanley was born in Denbigh in 1841 and the parish baptismal records identify him as the illegitimate son of John Rowlands and Elizabeth Parry.

Elizabeth worked in a Denbigh bakery close to the offices of a firm of lawyers in which James Vaughan Horne was a leading partner. Rowlands admitted paternity of the boy but contributed nothing to his upbringing and took no interest in him. It is said that John Rowlands was paid to say that he was the father. Certainly James Vaughan Horne would have been ruined by a scandal. He was not only a lawyer and town council worthy; he had also married into a prominent local family, the Prices of Llanrhaeadr Hall.

In the churchyard I read the epitaph on the tombstone of Ann Parry: Fe wirodd Duw ei air – God kept his word. Just before she died in 1787 she said she hoped her body would remain as incorruptible as her soul. More than forty years later her son was buried in the same grave and the gravedigger accidentally opened her coffin and found her perfectly preserved. He was so shocked he kept quiet about it, but three years later, burying the son's widow, he opened Ann Parry's coffin again. This time he reported that she was unchanged and a curious committee saw that he was right.

Walking beside the rushing Clwyd I recalled that our old friend Dr Johnson was contemptuous of it. Why sir, he said, I could leap over it. Of course, he was teasing. He couldn't have leapt over a puddle. And he was equally rude about the Clwydian mountains. Mole hills, he snorted.

The church at Llanynys kept a glorious secret until 1967. In that year the vicar noticed that the plaster was flaking and that

The hidden treasure of Llanynys

under it lay some painting. He had the plaster stripped away to reveal a wonderful mural of St Christopher carrying Christ on his shoulders across a river. It was painted six hundred years ago and is a picture full of life. The artist's little joke still makes you smile: the larky fish nibbling at St Christopher's bare toes.

It was not far to the church at Llanychan, which, although small, has an impressive pipe organ. Among the figures in the stained glass window is a surprisingly modern business-man. 'It's my father,' Mari-gold Graham explained to me. 'He's there with his first wife and his son Alan. He gave the window in thanks for count-less mercies. Firstly, his son survived the trenches in the First World War; secondly he was prosperous in business in

Stained glass thankyou

Liverpool; and thirdly he was able to save this church.

'It all came about when he met the Archbishop of Wales on a train to London and the Archbishop warned him that he would have to close the church. So my father said: "If I repair the roof, put in an organ and supply a choir will you keep the church open?" The Archbishop agreed there and then, on the train. So my father installed the organ and recruited the choir. I remember an advertisement in the newspaper saying: Chauffeur required, must have a good tenor voice.'

The Vale of Clwyd boasts its own special fruit, the Denbigh plum. Paul Chamberlain showed me a specimen in his garden. 'But the fruit doesn't last long. The only way to eat it is straight from the tree. The flavour is superb.'

I walked a sunken lane worn deep by centuries of feet to the church at Llangynhafal. David de Lloyd, a rector here in the seventeenth century, later became Dean of St Asaph and,

Pick and eat

as a tribute to his conviviality, composed his own memorial:

This is the epitaph
Of the Dean of St Asaph
Who by keeping table
Better than he was able
Ran into much debt
Which is not paid yet.

Plas-yn-llan, nearby, was loved by William Wordsworth. He spent idyllic summer days here with his old travelling companion Robert Jones, the son of the house, and found inspiration and contentment. He and Robert Jones went on a walking tour in France in 1790 and Wordsworth dedicated one of his early books to him.

I made my way through the thick ferns to the end of my walk on Moel Fammau, the highest point of the Vale of Clwyd. To mark the golden jubilee of George III in 1810, the people of Flint

William Wordsworth's happy days

and Denbigh raised the money to pay for a pillar to surmount the peak. It was intended to be 150 feet high but the funds ran out at 126 feet. In 1862 a storm blew it down.

The foundations, however, make a grandstand from which there are tremendous views, in one direction Liverpool, and in another the peaks of Snowdonia. They say that William Gladstone, the Prime Minister, climbed to the summit one sunny day, looked out over the Vale, took off his hat and cried: 'Well done, God!' To which you'll respond, if you walk up here, 'Amen.'

AUTHOR'S NOTE

Trevor Fishlock is an award-winning international journalist who has reported from more than seventy countries. He has been staff correspondent for *The Times* in New York and India, and *The Daily Telegraph*'s man in Moscow. His books include *Wales and the Welsh*, *Talking of Wales*, *India File*, *The State of America*, *Out of Red Darkness*, *My Foreign Country* and *Cobra Road*.

Wild Tracks is also available, featuring the following walks: Gower, Anglesey Coast, Taff Trail, Pembrokeshire Coast, Snowdon, Severn Valley, Gwent Borderland, Dysynni Valley, Wye Valley, Ystwyth Valley, Hiraethog Moors and Carmarthen Coast.